MEXICAN RECIPES
FOR THE
HOME COOK

TU CASA MI CASA

ENRIQUE OLVERA

LUIS ARELLANO
GONZALO GOÛT
DANIELA SOTO-INNES

PHOTOGRAPHS BY ARACELI PAZ

LEGEND

Dairy-free

DF

Gluten-free

GF

Vegan

V

Vegetarian

VEG

Less than 30 minutes

30

Less than 5 ingredients

5

FOREWORD

PETER
MEEHAN

We had probably been in the same room before. But I actually met Enrique Olvera for the first time when I showed up at his just-relocated and about-to-reopen restaurant Pujol, in Mexico City, to film a scene for a tv show.

There is a jittery disjointed feel to the hurry-up-and-wait timeline of TV -making and a pent-up pregame inertia to a restaurant opening. The mix could have been toxic. Instead, Enrique and his team were welcoming and easygoing, and they took time to explain things that I probably should have known walking in. They obliged requests for off-camera samples of Pujol's famous mole madre and served the entire crew glasses of rare and mezcals made from wild agaves during a lull in the shoot. When we'd finished and were scrambling to disappear, to stop taking up space, Enrique more or less told everybody to sit down and have a drink, to pay a little attention to the beauty of the late afternoon shadows in this never-eaten-in space, and to chill. "Relax," he instructed us. "You're in Mexico." He was being sincere. He said it with gravitas and warmth.

Enrique wanted us to honor the reality of where we were by breathing it in, by slowing down and paying attention. To maybe inhale a little of the centuries of histories that collided and intertwined to make the place, Mexico City, and its cuisine. To acknowledge this moment in time, which led him to open a taco-tasting-menu bar and for us to fly hundreds of miles to point our cameras at it. But he didn't spell it out in the dorky, didactic way that I just did: he talked about how the about-to-open restaurant would be calm in the afternoons and "sexy" at night.

Many of the "best in the world" chefs are extremely good at narrative. They talk in a cadence that will eventually be codified as some sort of cheftambic pentameter, a paragon of low-key self-glorification, that will be taught in courses about success in culinary schools. While Enrique is ardently engaged in the act of storifying his cooking in books and periodicals and conferences, this is not him. He leaves things unsaid, leaves unnecessary things out of the frame—or off the plate. Because at some point, he figured out that sitting in the afternoon and appreciating the shadows was important, too. Important to his trajectory, his success, his story, and the perception of his cooking.

When I pressed Enrique on the point, it seemed like opening his first New York restaurant, Cosme, was the turning point for him. That was when his knuckles weren't so white gripping the steering wheel. His journey—including the Culinary Institute of America and opening his own restaurant at twenty-four, which would become recognized as one of the best in the world—then entered a new phase. He came, he saw, he conquered. This was when he realized that as good as it is to be the Guy Who Can Do Everything, you can be plenty successful and maybe a little bit happier if you gather a group round the table and share what it holds.

And that was when Enrique's collaborators—the people who actually ran the restaurants—became his partners. Three of them are credited as coauthors of this book: Daniela Soto-Innes, who runs the show at the Olvera-affiliated New York restaurants Cosme and Atla; Luis Arellano, a longtime Pujol lieutenant who now helms Criollo in Oaxaca; and Gonzalo Goût, opening General Manager of Cosme and behind the bar Ticuchi, which is opening in the original Pujol space. In Mexico City. I think it's related that the recognition paid to his restaurants has soared, especially since Arellano and Soto-Innes were installed in their own respective kitchens and kingdoms. All three have lent their expertise and recipes to the pages herein, and have enriched the book.

The principle at work here—working between these covers and across North America, as Olvera continues to expand his empire—is that the family that eats together and cooks together eats better and lives better. This is the benefit of a big extended Mexican family, the kind he writes about in Food for Sharing, focused on foods for a birthday party or a Sunday afternoon when all the cousins are coming over. The Mexican-ness of the ideas behind Olvera's—and his partners'—cooking is primary. And that is why this is a book about Mexican cooking, about the foundation of what they do, rather than one that showcases all the exquisite little things they do to food at their restaurants. This is the wellspring of their outlook on food, these are the foods they make for themselves and their loved ones, shared in recipes that you (and I) can and will make.

Mexican eating has set rhythms, lilting and loose as they often are, that give shape to the reality of the cuisine. This book celebrates the recipes with the accompanying stories: that esquites (page 140) are what's eaten in a Mexican town plaza; the *churrería* is next to the park (because of course people want churros when walking in a park); beer is for drinking with a bowl of chilaquiles when you're hungover. (I mentioned a hangover to a waiter in Mexico City

and he brought me a beer, unrequested, before my chilaquiles were even ready.)

The rules of the Mexican home cooking cuisine, such as they are, come in the same camouflage: grandmotherly admonitions and nudges to do better. You will not make it through these pages with the feeling that an epazote-less kitchen is an acceptable place to be putting together dinner. To explain the primacy of salsa-making, Enrique writes, "People might not remember if the chicken was properly cooked, but they will most certainly remember the salsa it was cooked in." His grandma's line that blenders make sauces "taste like electricity" will haunt you, even if you can't prove it in a blind taste test.

In these pages, what seems like a well-put-together folio of Mexican dishes you know (and others you'd like to) is a covert look at the blueprint for Enrique's success, at its underlying truths. There's a simplicity to these recipes that can inspiration: what's left out here is as intentional as what's included. I am excited to spend more time with this book because as I return to it, I learn more each time—but always in passing, always casually, always like I'm across the table from Enrique himself.

Relax, he'd probably advise you, and it's good advice. And then it's time to head to the kitchen.

INTRODUCTION

ENRIQUE OLVERA

Cooking is simpler than it seems, especially if you love eating. Eating is delicious especially if you love good conversation. In my home, as in most of my country, we love to eat and converse, we therefore love to cook. With cooking, I not only set the tone for the conversation but the food becomes the topic itself. Cooking is a labor of nurturing love, of neighborly care. There is nothing more intimately beautiful in this world than to cook, for someone you love, their favorite meal, and vice versa.

When I cook, I hear music: I remember the doves, the sparrows, the stars, and all the other magical creatures of old songs. I invariably remember the afternoon light that came in through my childhood kitchen. Memory is a powerful ally when it comes to food. It helps us travel in time to the aromas and flavors of the cuisine of our childhood. Often, I am transported to my aunts' houses, my grandmother's dining room, my mom's kitchen table. As fresh as if they had been created yesterday, my food memories are always within reach: breakfast on Sunday with my parents and siblings, family gatherings full of stews, *chicharrón* in salsa, *pozole verde*, and of course rice. That same rice that would morph the next day, when topped with crema and put inside a freshly made warm tortilla, into an incomparable taco. My mouth is watering as I write this, just as a deep and precious nostalgia settles over this memory. Unlike with home cooking, this feeling seldom overcomes us when having a meal at a restaurant. Not because restaurant meals are not served with care and dedication, but rather because it is very difficult to replace the intimate nature of the hearth. *Sazón*—the incredibly personal magical seasoning powers everyone has—varies immensely from family to family. Home cooking is a very personal affair. It is a reflection of who we were, who we are, and even of who we do or don't want to be.

It is impossible then to separate our cooking from our family story, from the products from the region we grew up in, or the regions our ancestors hailed from. It is impossible not to carry, wherever your path leads you, the flavors you grew up with. These flavors travel well and know no borders. They travel time and place through word of mouth, an heirloom, a barely legible, falling-apart notebook. These flavors are meddlesome, resilient, and stubborn. No matter the length of the journey, they will always persevere. Because of this, they exist beyond just a craving. They take us to a place of serenity, safety, pride. Just a whiff of a homemade soup can make you feel as if everything is okay, that there is a place you belong to and a place that belongs to you. It is a hug.

Cooking is also magic. I have very vivid memories of my childhood, when I discovered how bread dough felt on my hands, and how different that was from the textures of water and flour on their own. Flavorwise too: when you are a child, how else other than magic, do you explain how bread can taste so good when flour and water are not nearly as appetizing on their own. I am still marveled by the number of forms a raw egg can transform into; still in awe at the beautiful strangeness of the octopus. I am still enchanted by the assertive pungency of the onion, the sneakiness of chiles, the gust of freshness from a handful of herbs. There is magic in the trips to the markets, where shopping lists complete themselves while chatting, often in double meanings with *marchantes* that have been selling there for longer than time can count. There is undeniable magic roaming through those hallways past the perfumes of mangos, and guavas or with a taste of *chicozapote* or a tostada with crema. At markets, you see the most intense colors in the world. To this day, the dried chile hallway in markets is one of my favorite aromas.

Cooking at home is about intuition: about coming back from the market and letting yourself be led by the desire to do things with care, generosity, and intent. Cooking at home is enjoying the process, taking time to taste, smell, and listen. It is lived through setting the table, shaping a flower arrangement, fixing a drink, playing music. It is a therapy of reconnecting and reconstructing the relationship with your self. By using external factors—the food, the market, the music—we can delve inside and celebrate who we are and where we come from. Cooking at home is offering the best of who you are, without thinking about it.

It is impossible to imagine Mexican cuisine without masa, salsas, beans, and the other essential elements you'll find in the following pages. These ingredients and recipes are the foundations of our cuisine. Added to any table or plate, they immediately make it Mexican: For example, if you serve simply grilled meat with tortillas and salsa you have tacos. The flavor profiles of our culinary cornerstones are deeply rooted in our culture and folklore, most dating back to pre-Hispanic or early colonial times. They have endured for centuries with very few changes, in spite of how different our society is today. We think that in Mexican culture (as in many others), these deeply ingrained flavor profiles and simple methods create deep and emotional connections to our heritage.

If you master these basics and make them your own, you will understand the essence of Mexican cooking; you will be able to build upon these foundations and add your own personal style.

BASICS

Masa and Corn

What is corn? Native to the Americas, *Zea Mays L.* is a domesticated grass of which modern varieties can grow up to seven feet (over two meters). It is an annual plant: It completes its life cycle, from being a seed to producing seeds, within a year. It is also an incredibly efficient plant, since from one seed it produces hundreds of new ones. Corn has two flowers that are both unisexual. Male flowers are the highest point in the stalk and female ones grow in the pits between the stalk and leaves. These female flowers produce a spike or ear full of seeds that we call the cob. Corn kernels need humans to detach them from the cob and sow each individual seed, so we have therefore become interdependent species.

Before humans started planting it, corn was a very different plant than it is today. Called *teosinte,* corn's ancestor only produces about ten little seeds that look like a geometric lentil, rather than like corn kernel. There is evidence that it was domesticated 3,000 years ago, and since then there have been numerous archeological digs that show us corn has evolved with humans on the Americas. Entire civilizations have made their life around corn. Mayans for example, believed that corn was more than an ingredient; it was part of the creation myth. In the *Popol Vuh,* the Mayan mythological "people's book," we learn that in their fourth try, the gods successfully made man out of corn and all peoples of the world descend from this first corn-derived human.

In its long history, corn has had two defining moments that have dramatically altered its course, and the course of civilizations. The first was the discovery of nixtamalization. The second was the conquest and subsequent export of corn to the world.

Nixtamalization is the process of cooking and then soaking corn kernels in an alkaline solution, either by adding cal (calcium hydroxide pickling lime) or wood ash to the cooking water. This alkaline solution peels the outer skin, or pericarp, of the corn so that it can be easily removed. The result is a corn that is much easier to work with, more malleable, and most crucially, with an easier access to nutrients. The grand Aztec and Mayan empires were based on a diet that relied on beans and nixtamalized corn, which when combined form a complete protein.

I believe—and I am not alone—that nixtamalization was discovered by chance. I think it occurred because someone accidentally added ash to their cooking water and when they went to grind the corn the next day, the dough was much easier to work with and they continued doing it and shared the knowledge. Nowadays, the process of making masa is understood much more, but the basics remain unchanged.

The second large leap that corn took was its travels abroad. The Nahuatl (Aztec) word for corn is actually *centli,* but the conquistadors encountered populations in the Caribbean and this

Aztec word was quickly discarded in Spanish in favor of its Antillean cousin, *mahis.* Five hundred years later, corn's high yield and ease of growth have made it the most planted crop on the planet. However, most of it goes to feedstock or industrial uses such as ethanol production. In most of the world, corn-as-food is not nixtamalized: It is eaten as a fresh vegetable or ground up, as cornmeal or grits.

To make masa (dough), nixtamalized corn is traditionally ground in a *metate*—a flat volcanic rock over which food is pressed with a rod-shaped rock. Although there are some very traditional cooks who still use the *metate,* most of the fresh masa comes from community *molinos* or mills, where two volcanic rocks attached to a mechanical mill spin to grind the corn. At our restaurants, we have installed a version of these in our kitchens. For grinding corn at home, you can find small, hand-cranked mills online. Keep in mind that they tend to be labor intensive and won't always produce the same results as the *molinos.* A food processor can also be used to grind the corn into masa. With this technique, you will need to add a lot of water in order to grind it properly. This means you need to dry out the masa to the right consistency afterward (see page 22 for drying instructions). Unfortunately, we have not found a practical technique that helps you make the perfect masa at home. As an alternative to making your own masa—as we know it is labor intensive—we recommend finding a local Mexican grocery store or community, where there might be a *molino* or *tortillería,* with high-quality masa. This is what most people in Mexico do when they make fresh tortillas at home.

Finally, masa harina, though not ideal, is quick and practical; and if it is all you have, it is still much better than supermarket-bought tortillas. Masa harina is the default shortcut that fits right in with modern urban life. In large cities, many *tortillerías,* for example, use it instead of freshly nixtamalized corn. Its biggest limitation, however, is the quality of the corn used to produce masa harina, as it tends to be fairly industrialized. There are over sixty types of heirloom corn that are regionally used to make masa and none are used for masa harina. The best tortillas, in other words, come from freshly nixtamalized and ground, preferably heirloom, corn.

Nixtamal and Masa

Preparation time
1 hour, plus overnight soaking

For the nixtamal
1 lb (455 g) dried corn,
  preferably heirloom
4 quarts (3.8 liters) water,
  plus more for milling
1 teaspoon (4 g) cal (aka
  calcium hydroxide or pickling
  lime)

▮DF ❀GF ◐V ♣VEG ⌂5

The yield of a pound of corn varies depending on the type of corn used. Heirloom varieties will yield about 1.5 pounds (680 g) of masa for every pound of corn, whereas commercial corn will yield about 2 pounds (910 g) of masa. We suggest using heirloom varietals, not only because it has a more complex flavor, but to support small independent farmers. We buy our corn and a few other corn-based products, from Masienda (masienda.com), a wonderful project that we recommend as the best source of heirloom corn outside of Mexico.

———

Make the nixtamal

1. Prepare the corn. Place the corn in a large container and add enough tap water to cover. This will eliminate any excess dirt, leaves, and cob pieces, which should float to the top. Drain and rinse the corn well.

2. In a pot, bring the 4 quarts of water to a boil and whisk in the cal (lime), dissolving completely. Add the corn. If the water is properly alkalinized, the tip of the kernels will turn yellow. If they don't turn yellow, add a bit more cal to the water, ¼ teaspoon (1 g) at a time.

Cook over high heat, stirring regularly, until the kernels are al dente (if you cut into a kernel, they should be translucent on the outside and opaque on the inside), 30–35 minutes. Remove from the heat, cover, and let rest overnight or for at least 7 hours. Do not refrigerate.

At this point, the outer skin will have begun to molt. Drain the mixture and rinse the corn in a colander, rubbing together to completely remove the outer skin. They should easily peel. Once the corn is shiny, it is ready to mill or grind.

Make the masa

3. Mill the corn following your chosen method (see page 20). The masa should be the texture of Play-doh; as it is milled, add enough cold water to make sure the dough passes through without burning the corn. Adjust the grind depending on how the masa will be used: Tortilla masa, for example, should be finer than tamal masa.

4. Before using, knead the masa with your hands and adjust the texture with water, it should be very malleable and tacky but not sticky. If it is too wet, place the masa in a bowl uncovered in the fridge and dry it out, at least 1 hour.

1.

2.

3.

4.

Tortillas, Tostadas, and Tlayudas

Tortillas and tostadas act as vessels, spoons, or sponges. They are similar to bread: A foundation that is wonderful on its own, and a practical and flavorful base for anything you might put on or in it. For example, Quesadillas (page 92) are as simple as tortillas with some melted cheese in them, yet they are such a satisfying snack.

A fresh tortilla made with good-quality corn can be an exquisite pleasure. Here are some pointers for making them. You need only four things: masa, two squares of plastic cut from a zip-seal plastic bag, a tortilla press, and a hot comal or frying pan. You could even do without the tortilla press and use a glass pie plate, or if you are feeling adventurous, you can press by hand, but this takes a lot of practice and craftsmanship.

Tortillas

Freshly ground masa
(page 22)

⏃DF ⏃GF ⏃V ⏃VEG ⏃30 ⏃5

Prepare a comal (see page 30). Check that your masa is the correct consistency. If you make a ball and squeeze it, the masa should not crack, it should have elasticity. It should be tacky but not sticky.

Place one plastic square on the bottom side of the tortilla press. With your hands, take enough dough to shape into a walnut-size ball. Place the ball in the center of the plastic on the tortilla press.

Place the other plastic square over the ball and close the press, adjusting pressure based on the desired thickness of the tortilla. If the masa sticks to the plastic, it's too wet. If it cracks, it's too dry. Adjust the masa if necessary. Wet masa can be refrigerated uncovered for at least 1 hour, to dry out. Dry masa can be hydrated with water.

Peel off the top plastic. Pick up the tortilla using the bottom plastic, invert onto your free hand and peel off the plastic with the other. Half of the tortilla should be on your hand with the other half hanging over.

With a swift sweeping motion, place the tortilla on a previously heated dry comal or heavy pan over medium-high heat. Cook until the edges dry up a bit and you can pick up the tortilla from its edges, about 15 seconds. Flip and cook for another 30 seconds or so. Flip again and place on the hottest part of your comal or pan. Cook until the tortilla starts to inflate, 30–45 more seconds. Flip one last time and cook until slightly browned on both sides, about 15 more seconds. Remove from the heat.

Working in batches, cook the rest of the tortillas and wrap in a cloth napkin as they come off the comal or pan. We like to hold the wrapped tortillas in a basket, or *tortillero*, to keep them hot for as long as possible.

Tostadas

Tostada means "toasted" and that is exactly what it is. A toasted tortilla. You can make them on the stovetop over indirect heat or on a baking sheet in an oven set to the lowest possible temperature—just cook until crunchy. In Oaxaca, the tortillas are toasted on a wire grate over a comal.

Tlayuda

Freshly ground masa
  (page 22)
Asiento (page 134)
Refried Beans Puree (page 67)
Optional toppings: quesillo
  (Oaxaca string cheese),
  avocado, greens of choice,
  Chorizo (page 84) or other
  meat
Salsa, for serving

❦GF ▶30 ⌂5

Texturally, somewhere between a tortilla and a tostada lives the *tlayuda*: It is not quite soft, not quite hard. However, it is much bigger than the tortilla. It is similar to a pizza in size and shape. The *tlayuda* is from Oaxaca, where it is a very popular street food and diners get to choose what they want on it—in addition to the basics. In that sense it is like a pizza too.

———

Follow the same procedure as for forming the tortillas (page 24) but use double or triple the amount of masa per ball. If you do not have a large enough tortilla press, you can also use a rolling pin to make it extra thin.

Cook the *tlayuda* as directed on the first two sides. Once you come to the second flip, leave the *tlayuda* on the comal for about 1 minute, it should start getting a little hard. Flip the last time and give it another 1–2 minutes there. These don't tend to inflate.

Once ready but while still on the comal, spread the *tlayuda* with some *asiento,* then spread thickly with some refried beans. If desired, top with *quesillo,* avocado, greens, and cooked chorizo or other cooked meat, such as *tasajo.*

Serve with salsa on the side.

Flour Tortillas

Tortillas de harina

Preparation time
20 minutes, plus resting time
Cooking time
3–4 minutes per tortilla
Makes about 24 tortillas

2 lbs/7 cups (910 g) all-purpose
  (plain) flour, plus more for
  dusting
1 teaspoon baking powder
1 tablespoon salt
½ cup (120 g) unsalted butter
1 cup (240 ml/8 fl oz) lukewarm
  whole milk
1 cup (240 ml/8 fl oz) lukewarm
  water

✦VEG

Although most of Mexico eats corn tortillas—and they're our personal favorite—flour tortillas are more common in the north of Mexico or are used for specific preparations, such as gringas (tacos al pastor with melted cheese), and homemade tortillas are a far cry from the shelf-stable flour tortillas sold in supermarkets. Fresh flour tortillas are quite a treat, with an incomparable texture, and making them at home requires much less infrastructure than corn tortillas. That said, flour tortillas are very different from corn tortillas, and they don't always work as a substitute. For example, soft preparations like Quesadillas (page 92) or Tongue Tacos (page 172) might work well with a flour tortilla, but chilaquiles or other fried preparations do not. This recipe comes from the family of David Linares, sous-chef at Pujol and from Nuevo León, one of Mexico's northern border states. They can be made with vegetable shortening but we prefer to use butter instead. When preparing these tortillas, make sure to let the dough rest. You can refrigerate the dough for up to a day or freeze for up to a month; just make sure to bring back to room temperature before rolling the tortillas.

___

In a large bowl, combine the flour, baking powder, and salt and use your hands to mix together. Add the butter and incorporate completely until the mixture is crumbly and uniform, about 5 minutes. Add the milk and water and mix until completely incorporated. The mixture should be the texture of Play-Doh. Transfer to a lightly floured surface and knead until the texture is smooth, 2–3 minutes. Portion and roll into ping-pong–size balls and place on a lightly floured tray or on the counter. Cover with a damp cloth and let rest for at least 1 hour at room temperature, or until the dough feels soft when poked (or overnight, covered with plastic, in the refrigerator).

Heat a dry frying pan or comal over high heat. Using a rolling pin, roll the balls into disks as thin as possible. Place on the frying pan or comal and cook for 1 minute. Flip and cook for 1 minute on the other side or until brown spots appear. Flip one last time and cook until there are light brown spots on both sides. Transfer to a cloth-lined basket and serve immediately.

Preparing the Comal

A comal is a flat or almost flat surface made of a heat-conducting material that is placed directly on the fire. Most people have aluminum or cast-iron *comales* at home that work well for reheating tortillas or other items, but to cook tortillas, we prefer clay. Clay *comales* are smooth on the top side but are still porous, so it needs to be seasoned before you can cook on it, especially if making tortillas. The process is very simple. Just dissolve cal (pickling lime) in water—in a ratio of 1 part cal to 4 parts water—and spread the liquid over the cold comal, creating a uniform layer all over. This fills the pores of the clay and creates a uniform surface that prevents food from sticking. Then just heat it up and, using a cloth, brush off any clumps or loose cal. Repeat the process every once in a while, as soon as tortillas begin to stick to the comal when you're making them.

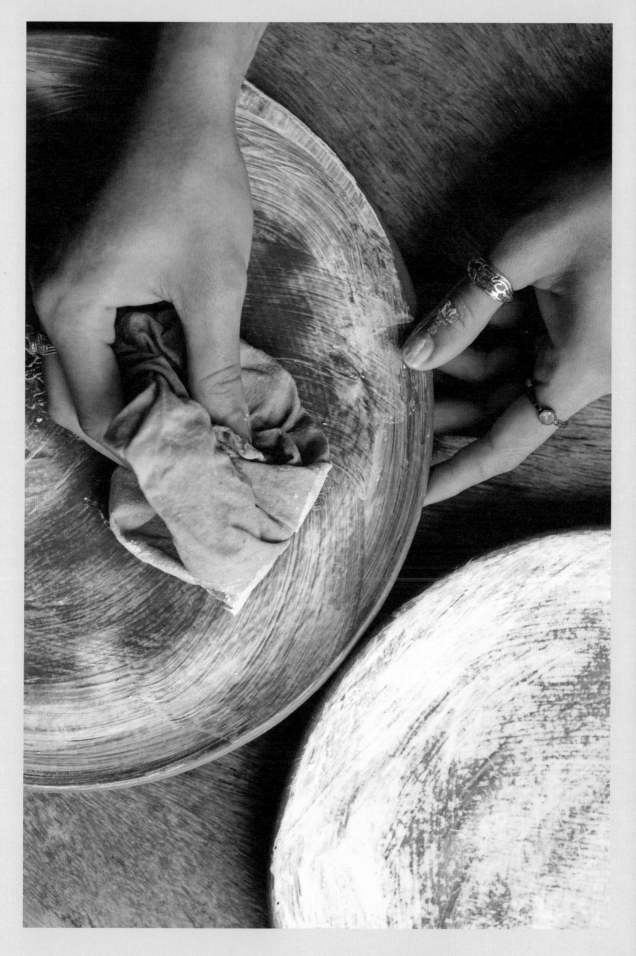

Tetela

Freshly ground masa
  (page 22)
Refried Beans (page 67)
Fresh hoja santa leaves
  (Mexican rootbeer leaf)
Shredded quesillo
  (Oaxaca string cheese)
Salsa and crema, for serving

♥ GF ✦VEG ▶30 ⛬5

Also from Oaxaca, *tetelas* are at the same time simpler than *tlayudas*—they have fewer ingredients—and more complex, as they are harder to assemble. Typically stuffed with just one or two components, they are closer to a quesadilla in that way. However, the ingenious wrapping of the masa makes this a perfect vessel to keep ingredients hot and it has the advantage of being a great to-go snack.

———

1. Adjust the texture of the masa if necessary, adding more water or allowing it to dry out (see page 22). Heat a comal or pan over high heat.

2. Follow the process for making tortillas (page 24) but use double or triple the amount of masa. Once you have evenly flattened the disk (flipping sides if necessary), remove the top plastic (keep the bottom plastic in place).

3. Add a spoonful of thick refried beans to the round of masa.

4. Add an hoja santa leaf and a handful of *quesillo*.

5. Picture a triangle going through the round. Take hold of the bottom plastic and fold one of the sides of the round up until the edge comes to the center of the round.

6. Fold in a second side to have both edges meet in the middle. It will be straight on two sides and round on the third, like a slice of pizza.

7. Fold the third side in, closing the triangle completely.

8. Carefully lift the *tetela* off the plastic, transfer to your free hand, and place on the comal or a hot pan.

9. Cook for about 1 minute on each side, until you have brown spots on both sides. Eat hot as is or cut a slit on the top side and add salsa and *crema*.

1.

2.

3.

4.

5.

6.

7.

8.

9.

Tamales

Tamales are a pre-Hispanic bundle of goodness fit for kings, literally. In the Aztec Empire, tamales were not only widely consumed by the populace but by the rulers as well. To this day tamales are still both a street snack and a dish worthy of serving to dignitaries at state dinners. Tamales are wonderful at any time of day, for breakfast or for supper as a savory snack or a sweet one. They can be eaten on their own or covered in beans. The range of possibilities for when and how tamales are consumed is outstanding.

In the kitchen, tamales are just as versatile: They are a vehicle for any number of fillings, and once you learn how to make a *tamal* and are familiar with the process, you can pretty much make tamales out of anything you like, beyond the common salsa and cheese varieties. You can use any of a variety of salsas (pages 46–58) or moles (pages 124, 126, 156 and 164) with cooked proteins such as chicken, pork, and beef. Or if you have leftovers, you can pop them in a *tamal*. Some overripe fruit? Go for it. The sky is the limit.

———

Some basics first

Wrapping: There are two basic wrappings used for tamales, and this has a lot to do with the flora of the region. The first wrapping is banana leaves, more commonly used in the south and southeast of Mexico. The other wrapping is dried corn husk, more commonly used in the central and northern areas of the country.

Filling: To fill a *tamal*, you have two options. The first option, as you will find in some recipes such as the Squash Tamales (page 200), is to combine a pureed ingredient with the actual masa. The second is to use the masa as is and add the filling of your choice.

Ratio of ingredients: The ratio of masa to other ingredients in the following basic recipe is approximate, as you should look for visual and taste cues. You can decide which fat to use based on the flavor it might add or based on dietary restrictions. The important thing is that it be at room temperature. For the liquid, you can use water or stock. For example, if you are filling the tamales with pork, you can use the broth the pork was cooked in. Some people also add baking powder to the masa for fluffier tamales. It is typically used more for corn husk tamales than for banana leaf ones.

Tamales should always be made in large quantities because of the amount of work and time involved in making them. If you don't have a big party coming up where you can serve a lot of tamales, you can always vacuum-seal and freeze them for up to three months or give the extra ones away.

Basic Tamal Recipe

Preparation time
30–40 minutes, plus masa preparation time and soaking time

Cooking time
1–1½ hours, plus filling cooking time

Makes about 20 tamales

20–25 banana leaves or dried corn husks

2 lb (910 g) freshly ground masa (page 22), at room temperature

1 cup (240 ml/8 fl oz) water, stock, or broth at room temperature

1 cup (240 ml/8 fl oz) fat, such as vegetable oil, coconut oil, lard, or butter, at room temperature

Puree of choice (optional)**

2 teaspoons salt, or to taste

2 teaspoons baking powder (optional)

Filling of choice (2–3 tablespoons per tamal)*

*We use a very simple Salsa Roja (page 50) and some cheese.

**Some tamal recipes add a puree to the masa; see Pineapple Tamales (page 198) and Squash Tamales (page 200).

**DF **GF **V **VEG

Prepare the wrappers

Find a big pot with a lid, a steamer with an insert/rack, or a *tamalera* (an aluminum pot specially designed to steam tamales).

If using corn husks, soak them in lukewarm water for 30–60 minutes, or until you can fold them against the grain without tearing. Soak about 10 percent more than you will use since some will always tear during the folding.

For banana leaves, pass all of them over an open flame about 4 inches away until they turn a lighter waxier green color. If you buy frozen banana leaves, this process will be very easy. Cut them into squares; they don't need to be perfect. We cut ours about 10 inches (25 cm), but you can adjust based on the size you would like your tamales. However, it's always better to have a larger square.

Prepare the masa

I. Whip or knead the masa and add liquid. In a mixer with a paddle attachment or using your hands, whip the masa with ½ cup (120 ml/ 4 fl oz) of the water or stock until it starts to come together instead of crumbling. If your masa is at room temperature, it will happen more quickly.

With the mixer running, stream in more of the water or stock, whipping until you reach the consistency of hummus or cake batter. This can take anywhere from 3–5 minutes.

2. Whip fat into the masa. Incrementally add the room-temperature fat to the masa and keep whipping. Add fat until you can see the masa get shiny. If adding a puree, this is when you would add it to flavor the masa. Keep whipping for about another 3 minutes to emulsify properly. The final consistency should be of smooth puree or thick sour cream. Add more liquid and fat if needed. Season with salt. If using, this is when you would add the baking powder.

Shape the tamales

3. Portion the masa and filling. Line up the banana leaves on a work surface with the opaque side of the leaf facing up. Using a large spoon, evenly portion the masa among them. If each banana leaf was a tic-tac-toe board, the masa should mostly be in the center square. We add 3–4 tablespoons of masa to each, but you can make them larger if desired. Make a little crater in the center of the masa with the spoon. (For corn husks: Line up the corn husks on a work surface with the narrow end of the husk pointing toward you. Portion the masa closest to the wider end of the husk, where it was attached to the corn cob.)

4. Add 2–3 tablespoons of the filling to each *tamal.* If you decide to make them larger, add some more.

1.

2.

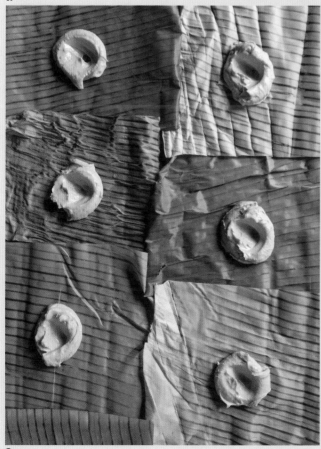

3.

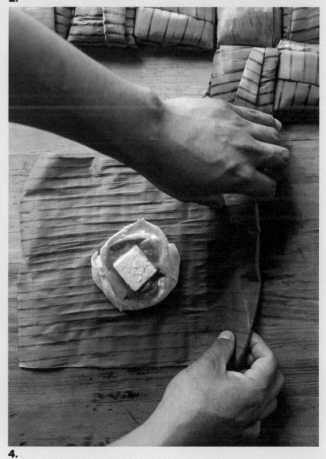

4.

5. Wrap the *tamal* (banana leaves). Start by folding the top one-third of the banana leaf toward the center.

6. Fold the bottom third toward the center. Fold the edge back a bit if it is too long and keep the masa tightly in the center holding the leftover flaps with both hands.

7. Flip it over, taking care to keep the masa in place, seam side down.

8. Keeping the masa tightly in the center, fold the two leftover flaps into the middle. Flip the tamal over again, flap side down, while you wrap the rest of the tamales. (For corn husks: Just wrap in the two sides following the husk's natural shape and form and then fold the tip of the husk up toward the wide end. For some more stability and/or for prettier presentation, you can use strips of husk to tie the *tamal*, but the two ends of the husk remain open.)

Prepare the pot

If using a *tamalera* or a steamer pot, add enough water to reach, but not touch, the insert. If using a regular pot, place a metal colander upside down at the bottom of the pot and add 2–3 inches (5–7.5 cm) water.

Place the tamales (banana leaves) in the pot, seam side down and in concentric circles. Whenever you are ready to start another layer, intersperse them over the cracks of the previous layer, instead of on top of another *tamal*. (For corn husk tamales: These are cooked "standing up" with the open ends up, so insert them in the pot with the fold side down.)

Cook the tamales

Tightly cover the pot and steam the tamales for 1–1.5 hours. (Corn husk tamales will cook in the same time.) Just take care that the water doesn't completely evaporate or the bottom of the pot will burn and make the tamales stink. Add more boiling water as needed. The tamales will still be soft even though they are fully cooked. Take one of the tamales from the pot and unwrap it. The dough should not stick to the leaves when you do.

The tamales must rest for at least 30 minutes so they can set. You can reheat them later if necessary, but if you try to eat them right out of the pot, the inside will still be runny.

5.

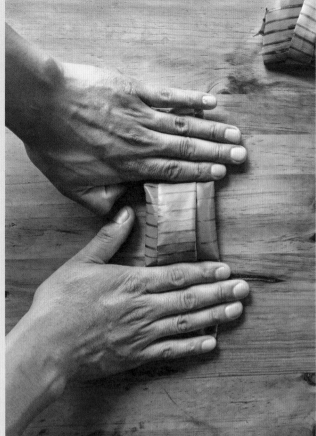

6.

7.

8.

Tlacoyo

Preparation time
1 hour, plus overnight soaking
and salsa preparation time

Cooking time
5–10 minutes

Serves 6–8

For the split peas
½ lb (225 g) dried split peas,
soaked overnight in room-
temperature water

For the split pea puree
2 tablespoons lard or grapeseed
oil
3 large garlic cloves, sliced
10 fresh or dried avocado leaves
3 dried morita chiles, seeded
and deveined
1 teaspoon salt

For the tlacoyos
2 lb (910 g) Freshly ground
masa (page 22)
Grapeseed oil, for shallow-
fryingt
1 cup (230 g) crema or crème
fraîche, at room temperature,
for serving
1 cup (120 g) crumbled queso
fresco, at room temperature,
for serving
1 cup (235 g) Raw Salsa Verde
with Peas (page 46), for
serving

⟡GF ♦VEG

Tlacoyos, eye-shaped thick tortillas with various fillings, are romantic and practical. Romantic because they remind all Mexicans of the ubiquitous street *tlacoyo* and quesadilla vendor, typically a woman who makes and sells them out of her *anafre*, a street griddle. Practical because they are one of the few masa-based foods that is cooked twice, allowing you to make them ahead of time and just fry and garnish—with cream cheese and salsa—right before serving. This split pea filling is less common, but you can make *tlacoyos* with any variety of fillings. The filling must be cooked down to a thick paste, whether refried black beans (page 67), *requesón* (page 82), or dried fava (broad) beans.

———

Cook the split peas: Drain the peas and place in a large pot. Add water to cover by 2 inches (5 cm) and bring to a simmer. Cook covered over low heat until very soft, 1½–2 hours. Drain excess liquid. Measure out 1⅓ cups (250 g) of the cooked peas and set aside.

Make the puree: In a small pot, heat the lard or oil over medium heat and cook until golden brown, about 1 minute. Add the garlic and cook for 2 minutes. Add the avocado leaves and morita chiles and cook for 1 minute. Add the reserved peas and cook for 3 minutes. Add the salt and remove from the heat. Transfer the ingredients to a blender or food processor and blend until uniform but still a bit chunky. Add a little water or more cooked split peas if necessary; the puree should be fairly thick. Allow to cool to room temperature.

Make the tlacoyos: Using your hands, portion and shape the masa into balls slightly larger than a golf ball. Cover with a wet paper towel. Flipping the masa back and forth between your hands, shape it into a disk ¼–½ inch (6–12.5 mm) thick. Cup with one hand and with the other carefully place at least 2 tablespoons pea puree in the center. Cup the disk of masa in both hands and fold the opposite sides toward the center, enclosing the filling, with the seam running down the middle. Press the seam to close. You should have a shape similar to a rugby ball. Press slightly to flatten, keeping the seam on one of the flat sides. Further flatten the *tlacoyo* by slapping it back and forth between your hands until it's ¼–½ inch (6–12.5 mm) thick and the shape of an eye. Make as many tlacoyos as the masa or the puree yield, keeping a 2:1 ratio of masa to puree.

Heat a comal or large pan over medium heat. Cook the *tlacoyos* for about 1 minute per side, flipping three times, until lightly browned. You can prepare the *tlacoyos* through this step ahead of time. If you are making them the day before, wrap in a tea towel and then in a plastic bag and refrigerate.

In a small frying pan, heat ¼–½ inch (6–12.5 mm) oil over medium-high heat. Cook the *tlacoyo* for 1 minute per side. Transfer to paper towels to drain. Top with salsa, *crema*, and queso fresco.

Salsas

To understand salsas, grab a frying pan or comal and throw in two tomatoes, a clove of garlic, a fresh chile, and some onion and let them cook. Char them. There are no measurements for how much or how long to cook them for. The salsa will be yours at whatever point you stop charring and decide it is ready. You cannot screw it up. Throw the ingredients in a blender or into a *molcajete* (volcanic stone mortar, page 45) and add some salt. Put the salsa on a tortilla, meat, or a slice of cheese, or eat directly with a spoon. You will find that salsas are the very essence of our cuisine. They are simple and yet exquisite.

People might not remember if the chicken was properly cooked, but they will most certainly remember the salsa it was cooked in. We return to our favorite *taquerías* not because of what is in the taco but because of the salsas. At every restaurant, salsas are the first thing to be brought to the table, if they are not already there.

In the home kitchen, salsas are a true staple and an everyday pleasure. Every refrigerator in the country has at least one container with salsa in it at any given moment. The tough part is deciding what salsa to make. It's a huge game of variations. Raw, charred, or boiled? With tomato or tomatillo? Dried chiles or fresh? Herbs or spices? As a home cook, salsas are a very personal affair. The more you make them, the more you set yourself in your ways. The more you perfect your salsa, the less eager you'll be to start crafting a new one. Usually a cook perfects a couple of salsas and sticks to them. Every household has one or two that is theirs and theirs alone. At my brother's house, they add a bit of cumin to their salsa verde and fry all the salsa after it is blended. A friend fries the onions slowly for a long time and in plenty of oil before any of the other salsa verde ingredients are added. The repertoire of unique salsas that every Mexican has is quite vast. You should make your own salsas and experiment with chiles and ingredients until you have found yours.

The Three Main Elements of Salsa

Chiles. Chiles are the most important element of salsas. The variety of chiles we have just in Mexico is mind-blowing. Ricardo Muñoz Zurita—a dear friend, wonderful chef, and researcher of Mexican gastronomy like no other—published a 250-plus-page book just on Mexican chiles. Chiles are consumed both fresh and dried and sometimes, like chipotles or pasilla mixe, they are smoked and sometimes preserved in adobo (like canned chipotles). Each has a particular flavor, level of heat, and tradition behind it. When the dried or smoked chiles are used, they are typically toasted before being either hydrated in water or crushed directly into the salsa. When preparing chiles, you should always remove the stems. Ribs or veins and the attached seeds are the spiciest part of the chile. The seeds and ribs are typically removed except when you want a much higher level of spice, like with chile de árbol, or when the seeds are used for a preparation on their own, like the *mole chichilo* from Oaxaca, a resourceful specialty made out of charred seeds. Be careful when handling chiles to not touch your eyes and nose—or any other sensitive body part—until you have washed your hands. We've all learned that lesson the hard way.

Tomato (jitomate), tomatillos (tomate), and purplish heirloom tomatillos (miltomate). Not all salsas have tomatoes or tomatillos, but a vast majority do. Although you can find both in the same salsa, you will typically just see one or the other. A tomato-based salsa tends to be called *salsa roja* (red) and a tomatillo-based one is *salsa verde* (green). The root of both tomato and tomatillo is the same, from the Nahuatl word *tomatl*, which comes from *tomal* = plumpness or fatness and *atl* = water. However, they are different species and therefore have quite different flavors. Tomatoes are more water laden and their flavor is fruitier. Tomatillos are tart and crisp with an occasional faint jammy sweetness. *Miltomates* or *tomate de milpa* are a smaller, earthier version of tomatillos, generally harvested from wild plants growing among the cornfields or *milpas*. It is important to find ripe and good-quality produce, otherwise salsas will be watery and not very flavorful. Also, the papery husks of tomatillos should always be removed and the waxy flesh thoroughly rinsed.

Aromatics. The most common aromatics, by far, are onion (raw or cooked) and garlic (almost always cooked). Some salsas have both and some have just one or the other. As a matter of fact, when a salsa does not have tomatoes or tomatillos, it will invariably be made with garlic. You'll also find herbs, with cilantro (coriander) being the most common one, especially in salsa verde. Other additions might include spices, such as allspice; seeds and nuts, such as peanuts and sesame seeds; and even insects, like the highly sought after Mexican chicatana ants and agave worms.

The Molcajete

How to Season. *Molcajetes* are large mortars carved from dark, heavy volcanic basalt rock. They are used in the preparation of several Mexican condiments, especially salsas. They are fairly easy to find, but you should always look for one carved out of stone (the pores look irregular) rather than one constructed from a mold. Natural *molcajetes* need to be seasoned before using them for the first time, as the carving typically leaves a harsh surface that can chip when cooking. To season it, use the pestle to grind a handful of dried corn until it becomes a powder, making sure you grind over all surfaces inside the bowl. Discard the corn powder, rinse the *molcajete* using a thick-bristled brush, and let it air-dry. Next, add a handful of dried rice and repeat the same process as with the corn. Then do the same but with wet rice (just add one to two tablespoons of water to the *molcajete* bowl with the rice). At the end of this, the rice should not be gray. If it is, repeat the process. Finish by grinding just coarse salt and a clove of garlic. Brush off under running water and you are ready to use it. Once seasoned, and after each use, you should only wash it with water and salt, not soap. Unlike the comal, you only need to season a molcajete before the first use.

Making Salsa in a Molcajete. Although blenders are commonly used to prepare salsas, traditionally they are made with the *molcajete.* My grandmother said that salsas made in a blender taste like electricity. If you do not own a *molcajete,* we strongly suggest getting one. This volcanic rock mortar and pestle adds a layer of complexity to salsas that you will not be able to get from a blender. *Molcajetes* evolve as you use them, storing the *sazón* or seasoning of each cook with each use. When making a salsa on the *molcajete,* start with the harder-to-grind ingredients like the garlic, spices, and chiles. Add salt, preferably coarse sea salt, to this first process to help create grinding traction. Then add the onion and end with the tomatoes or tomatillos, bursting one at a time. You can leave it as chunky as you like. In order not to bruise herbs like chopped cilantro (coriander), we add them at the end, but you can add them with the onion if you like. Another great thing about the *molcajete* is that you just replace the pestle with a spoon and serve your salsa right out of it: It is a gorgeous serving vessel.

Salsas Verdes
Salsas verdes

Salsa verde is defined by the fact that it is made with tomatillos, which lend it a particular tart acidity, earthy sweetness, and thicker texture. Raw tomatillos and cooked ones have totally different attributes. They are both prized for the unique characteristic they bring to a dish. Raw salsa freshens and brightens heavier dishes such as fried masa, *Tlacoyos* (page 40) for example. However, this salsa tends to break when cooked. Cooked salsa, on the other hand, is uniform in its thicker texture and, while still providing acidity, highlights the jammy earthiness of the tomatillos.

Raw Salsa Verde
Salsa verde cruda

Preparation time
5 minutes
Makes
2 cups (475 ml/16 fl oz)

5 large tomatillos, husked, washed, and quartered
¼ large white onion
2 serrano chiles, or to taste
1 garlic clove, charred with the skin on and then peeled
½ cup (20 g) chopped fresh cilantro (coriander)
Salt, to taste

🍽DF 🥬GF 🌱V 🍀VEG ▶30

Salsa *cruda* (raw) is very easy to make and customize. To ensure a bright green color, have all ingredients well chilled. Raw salsas don't hold very well as their main attribute is their freshness. Make them as close as possible to serving.

———

In a blender, pulse all the ingredients to barely achieve a chunky consistency. (Alternatively, place all ingredients in a *molcajete*, starting with the garlic and salt, and mash until chunky.) Season to taste.

Variations
Raw Salsa Verde with Peas (*Salsa verde cruda con chícharos*): Add 1 cup cooked fresh peas. You can mash them a bit with a fork before adding them to the *salsa verde cruda*.

Raw Salsa Verde with Cucumber and Mint (*Salsa verde cruda con pepino y menta*): Add 1 cup peeled and chopped cucumber and 4 tablespoons chopped fresh mint.

Raw Salsa Verde with Avocado (*Salsa verde cruda con aguacate*): Add the flesh of 1 large avocado.

Cooked Salsa Verde

Salsa verde cocida

Photo p. 49

Preparation time
5 minutes

Cooking time
15–20 minutes

Makes
1½–2½ cups (355–590 ml/
12–20 fl oz)

5 large tomatillos, husked
 and rinsed
¼ large white onion
2 fresh serrano chiles, or to
 taste
1 garlic clove, unpeeled
½ cup (20 g) chopped fresh
 cilantro (coriander)
Salt, to taste

⦿DF ⦿GF ⦿V ⦿VEG ⦿30

You can make cooked salsa by charring the ingredients over heat or simmering them in water. The flavor profile is obviously very different. Charring gives you a smoky concentrated flavor that is perfect for salsas used as condiments. Water-cooked salsas tend to be better options for stews or longer cooking times.

———

Charred: Place a comal or frying pan over high heat. Place the tomatillos, onion, serranos, and garlic on the hot comal and char on all sides, about 20 minutes. Remove from the heat and cool to room temperature. Transfer all the charred ingredients to a *molcajete* or blender, add the cilantro (coriander) and salt to taste, and blend until chunky. Serve at room temperature or store in an airtight container in the refrigerator for up to 1 week.

Simmered: Peel the garlic. In a medium pot, combine the tomatillos, onion, serrano, and garlic. Add enough water to cover the ingredients and simmer over medium heat until the tomatillos are a pale green, 10–15 minutes, taking care to not let the water boil so they don't burst. Drain and let cool to room temperature. Transfer to a blender and pulse until broken down. Add the cilantro (coriander) and salt to taste, and blend until smooth. You can serve right away or fry in a hot pot with some vegetable oil. Serve warm or at room temperature, or store in an airtight container in the refrigerator for up to 1 week, or in the freezer for up to 1 month.

Mixe Chile Salsa

Preparation time
5 minutes

Cooking time
25 minutes

Makes
1 cup (240 ml/8 fl oz)

4 Mixe chiles, seeded
20 small firm tomatillos,
 husked and rinsed
2 large garlic cloves, unpeeled
1 teaspoon salt, or to taste

⦿DF ⦿GF ⦿V ⦿VEG ⦿30 ⦿5

Chile mixe or *pasilla oaxaqueño* is not to be confused with *pasilla mexicano*. The latter is long, up to 10 inches (25 cm), black in color, has very little heat and a deep earthy chocolate flavor. *Pasilla oaxaqueño*, or Mixe, is short, with a reddish hue, and has an incredibly fruity, smoky flavor. You only find the smoked chile in certain markets in the city of Oaxaca and at a couple of specialty stores abroad. If you manage to find a *pasilla oaxaqueño*, you will cherish it deeply. The Mixe people of Oaxaca are the only ones who grow and smoke the chile. Once it is smoked, its seeds are sterile, and it cannot be used to grow more chiles. It is impossible to come across this chile in its fresh form.

———

Heat a frying pan or comal over high heat. Add the chiles, tomatillos, and garlic. Remove the chiles once they brown on both sides, about 2 minutes. Continue to cook the other ingredients until charred on all sides, 15–20 minutes. Peel the garlic. In a *molcajete,* grind the garlic and salt to a paste. Add the chiles and finely grind. Add the tomatillos and grind into a watery paste. Adjust the salt and serve.

Cooked Salsa Verde

Salsas Rojas

Salsas rojas

Although a lot of salsas rojas can be used as a condiment, like pico de gallo or a simple salsa *ranchera*, many others are at the base of most *guisados* (stews). They are one of the most commonly found preparations in any of the regional cuisines of the country. Some people like to peel the tomatoes but we do not. We feel that it removes too much of the tomato's flavor.

Salsa Roja or Ranchera

Salsa roja o ranchera

Cooking time
25–30 minutes
Makes
2 cups (475 ml/16 fl oz)

6 plum (or heirloom) tomatoes
¼ large white onion
2 serrano chiles, or to taste
1 large garlic clove
Salt

ⅰDF ⅿGF ⅾV ⅿVEG Ɗ30 ⅿ5

This very basic salsa is sometimes called *ranchera*. It is so easy to make that it can be prepared out in the fields with minimal utensils and ingredients, rancher-style. We love it charred, but it can be simmered too. It is typically made with plum tomatoes but you can use other kinds, just make sure they are very ripe. We love to use fresh and ripe heirloom tomatoes whenever possible.

———

Heat a frying pan or comal over high heat. Place the tomatoes, onion, serranos, and garlic on the pan and char on all sides, about 20 minutes. Remove from the heat, let cool to room temperature, and mash in a *molcajete* or pulse in a blender until chunky. Serve at room temperature or refrigerate up to 1 week.

Salsa Roja with Dried Chiles

Salsa roja de chiles secos
Photo p. 51

Preparation time
15 minutes
Cooking time
25 minutes
Makes
2 cups (475 ml/16 fl oz)

4 tablespoons grapeseed oil
2 garlic cloves, sliced
¼ large white onion,
 roughly chopped
7 plum tomatoes, quartered
3 pasilla mexicano chiles,
 seeded
2 morita chiles, seeded
1 teaspoon salt, or to taste

ⅰDF ⅿGF ⅾV ⅿVEG

You can use any variety of chiles here. If you find a local spice store with a good variety, try out different ones and you will eventually narrow in on your favorites. These two chiles—pasilla and morita—are earthy and smoky. Although morita carries some heat, this is not necessarily a very spicy salsa.

———

In a medium pot, combine 2 tablespoons oil, the garlic, and onion and cook over medium heat until soft and translucent, about 3 minutes. Add the tomatoes and chiles and cook until soft, about 10 minutes. Add the salt and remove from the heat. Transfer to a blender and blend until smooth.

In a medium pot, heat the remaining 2 tablespoons oil over medium-high heat. Add the mixture and fry until it changes color to a garnet orange, 5–10 minutes. Serve warm or at room temperature, or store in an airtight container in the refrigerator for up to 1 week; or freeze for up to 1 month.

Salsa Roja with Dried Chiles

Árbol Chile Salsa

Salsa de chile de árbol

Preparation time
10 minutes

Cooking time
20 minutes

Makes
2 cups (475 ml/16 fl oz)

4 tablespoons grapeseed oil
24 chiles de árbol
6 garlic cloves, sliced
½ large white onion, quartered
5 plum (or heirloom) tomatoes, quartered
2 teaspoons salt, or to taste

DF GF NV VEG 30

This is quite a spicy salsa. The color is a beautiful, deep brick orange. If you would like to make this salsa spicier, leave the seeds in the chile de árbol. If you would like it even spicier, omit the tomatoes. Chiles de árbol are fairly common chiles, but you could also choose from a host of other spicy, but rarer, chiles such as *puya*, *tuxta*, *piquín*, *chiltepín*, or *comapeño* for this recipe.

———

In a medium pot, heat the oil over medium-high heat. Add the chiles and cook until bright red and crispy, 1–2 minutes. Using a large slotted spoon, transfer them to a bowl or plate.

Add the garlic and onion to the pot and cook until translucent, about 5 minutes. Add the tomatoes and cook until the tomatoes are mushy, another 10 minutes. Reduce the heat level if necessary, as nothing should brown. Return the chiles to the pot and cook until the flavors meld, about 2 minutes more, then remove from the heat.

Transfer to a blender, add the salt, and blend until smooth. Serve warm or at room temperature, or refrigerate in an airtight container for up to 1 week.

Pico de Gallo (or Salsa Mexicana)

Pico de Gallo (o salsa mexicana)
Photo p. 53

Preparation time
10 minutes

Makes
2 cups (475 ml/16 fl oz)

5 large plum or heirloom tomatoes
1 small white onion
½ bunch cilantro (coriander), with stems
2 fresh chiles de árbol, or to taste (you can substitute a jalapeño or serrano)
Salt

DF GF NV VEG 30 5

This term is used to refer to a fresh salsa that can be made with a variety of chopped fresh fruits or vegetables, sweet or savory, and can be served as a condiment, accompaniment, appetizer, or even a salad. The most common version in Mexico and abroad is this one, with tomatoes (red), onion (white), and the fresh (green) chile of your choice. It is called Mexicana because it has the colors of our flag. This salsa is made by chopping all of the ingredients rather than mashing or blending them. A lot of people like to add some Key lime juice to the salsa, but we feel the acidity of the tomatoes is enough to carry the salsa through.

———

Finely (or to your preference) chop the tomatoes, onion, and cilantro (coriander) leaves and stems. Mince the chiles. Combine everything in a bowl and season to taste with salt. Add more chile if you would like it spicier. Prepare as close to serving as possible.

Pico de Gallo (or Salsa Mexicana)

Other Salsas

Otras salsas

Pumpkin Seed Salsa

Ha' sikil pa'k

Preparation time
10 minutes
Cooking time
15 minutes
Makes
2 cups (475 ml/16 fl oz)

½ cup (65 g) pepitas (hulled
   pumpkin seeds)
3 plum tomatoes
1 tomatillo, husked and rinsed
¼ small white onion
6 garlic cloves
1 fresh chile de árbol or
   Thai chile
4 guajillo chiles, seeded
1 tablespoon salt, or to taste

▫DF ♡GF ◉V ♦VEG ◕30

Here are three more complex salsas that have additional ingredients beyond the usual suspects. These are almost always used as a condiment, due to their intense and particular flavor.

This pumpkin seed salsa is typical of Yucatán. Its name in Mayan lists the ingredients it has: *ha'*= water, *sikil* = pepitas, *pa'k* = tomato. It is a great salsa to serve with tostadas before a meal or to have as a snack with vegetables since its consistency is more of a spread than a liquid salsa. Adjust the level of heat to your taste.

———

Preheat the oven to 350°F (180°C/Gas Mark 4).

Place the pumpkin seeds on a baking sheet and toast in the oven until slightly golden, about 3 minutes. On a separate baking sheet, place the tomatoes, tomatillo, onion, garlic and the fresh chile. Cover with foil or a lid and bake until soft, 10–15 minutes.

Meanwhile, in a frying pan or over an open flame, lightly toast the guajillos, about 30 seconds on each side, taking care not to burn them or they will be bitter. Place them in a bowl and cover with room-temperature water to hydrate them, about 5 minutes. Reserving the soaking water, drain the chiles.

In a blender, combine the pumpkin seeds, tomatoes, tomatillo, onion, garlic, chiles, and salt and blend until smooth. Add a bit of the soaking water to achieve the consistency of a thick puree or dip, like hummus. Serve at room temperature or refrigerate in an airtight container for up to 1 week.

Peanut Salsa

Salsa con cacahuate

Preparation time
15 minutes
Cooking time
10–15 minutes
Makes
2 cups (475 ml/16 fl oz)

1¼ cups (295 ml/10 fl oz)
    grapeseed oil
4 pasilla chiles, seeded
15 chiles de árbol, seeded
1 ancho chile, seeded
6 puya or guajillo chiles, seeded
2 morita chiles
2 garlic cloves, peeled
1 cup (145 g) roasted peanuts
1 tablespoon salt, or to taste
Juice of 2 Key limes
½ cup chopped fresh cilantro
    (coriander)

DF GF V VEG 30

This is a chunky salsa that is surprisingly versatile, not only with Mexican foods but with a range of other dishes as well. It is a fresh variation of a *salsa macha*, a chunky, oil-based salsa that is always eaten as a condiment. If you do not add the Key lime and cilantro (coriander), this is a shelf-stable salsa: You can keep it in the pantry and use the flavored oil to cook with or use the chunky peanuts as a spicy topping.

———

In a small pot, heat the oil over medium heat until very hot but not smoking. Working one at a time and using tongs, fry the chiles for no more than 2–3 seconds each. Transfer to paper towels. After all chiles have been fried, fry the garlic until golden brown, 3–4 minutes. Reserve the oil.

Transfer the chiles, garlic and oil to a blender or a food processor and add the peanuts and salt. Blend until the peanuts are coarsely chopped. Transfer to a bowl and allow to cool to room temperature. Right before serving, mix in the Key lime juice and cilantro (coriander). Adjust the salt to taste.

Bone Marrow Salsa

Salsa con tuétano

Preparation time
10 minutes
Cooking time
20 minutes
Makes
2 cups (475 ml/16 fl oz)

1 lb (455 g) beef marrow bones
2 cups (230 g) thickly sliced
   white onion
5 habanero chiles (seeded
   for a less spicy version)
1 tablespoon salt, or to taste

ⒾDF ✌GF ◗30 ⌂5

In Yucatán, there is a very popular oil-based habanero salsa that is sometimes called black gold since the habaneros and the onion are charred until dark brown/black and then pureed with oil. This is a take on that salsa. Instead of using oil, we use bone marrow for a richer taste and texture. This salsa will be spicy, but if you want it at its spiciest, leave the seeds in the habanero. Enjoy on a tortilla or on top of tacos, such as the tongue tacos on page 172.

———

Preheat the oven to 400°F (200°C/Gas Mark 6).

Place the bones, onion, and habaneros on a baking sheet and roast until caramelized, about 15 minutes.

Scoop the marrow out of the bones into a blender. Add the charred onions, charred habaneros, and salt. Blend until smooth and serve hot. To reheat, warm in a frying pan or saucepan over low heat until the bone marrow fat starts to shimmer.

Escabeche

Escabeche

Preparation time
15 minutes
Cooking time
20 minutes
Makes
about 2½ quarts (2.4 liters)

½ cup (20 g) fresh thyme leaves
10 bay leaves
10 black peppercorns
½ cup (120 ml/4 fl oz) extra
    virgin olive oil
1 small white onion, sliced
8 small garlic cloves, peeled
¾ cup (115 g) cubed (2-inch/5
    cm) fresh pineapple
    (optional)
1 cup (125 g) sliced carrots
1 cup (125 g) baby potatoes
1 cup (90 g) sliced jalapeño
    chiles
2 cups (475 ml/16 fl oz) distilled
    white vinegar
2 tablespoons salt, or more
    to taste
½ small head (125 g) of
    cauliflower florets

DF GF V VEG

Although not technically a salsa, we decided to add escabeche to this section because, similar to salsas, it is a condiment that adds flavor and spice (heat) to dishes. Escabeche is a classic pickling recipe, widely used in Mexico for jalapeños. Escabeche is the actual pickling method, and although there are many things prepared and sold in escabeche—and you can make your own mix too—the vast majority of the escabeche found in Mexico is jalapeño-heavy, with varying amounts of other vegetables in it. We like to add the pineapple as a tangy and sweet contrast to the other flavors and textures. You can serve this to eat on its own along with *botanas*, or snacks, or you can add the jalapeños to a *torta*, the most common use for them (see Fish Milanese Torta, page 112). You can also preserve escabeche by using your preferred canning technique.

———

In a small frying pan, toast the thyme, bay leaves, and peppercorns, stirring constantly, until fragrant, 1–2 minutes. Set aside.

In a large pot, heat the oil over high heat until shimmering. Add the onion and garlic and cook until translucent, about 5 minutes. Add the toasted herb mix. Add the pineapple (if using), carrots, potatoes, and jalapeños and cook until fragrant, about 2 minutes. Add the vinegar and salt. Then add enough water to just cover the vegetables and bring to a boil. Boil for 1 minute, then reduce the heat to a soft simmer and cook until the potatoes are almost cooked but not quite, 7–8 minutes. Add the cauliflower and cook until the cauliflower is crisp-tender, 4 more minutes. Remove from the heat. Cool to room temperature and adjust the salt; the escabeche should be on the salty side. Store in the refrigerator for up to 1 month.

Beans

Beans *(frijoles)*, along with chiles and corn, make up the foundation of our cuisine and our diet. You will absolutely always find beans in a Mexican kitchen. We are pretty simplistic when it comes to beans. While we have a great diversity of heirloom bean varieties, which vary from region to region, they are all generally prepared in the same way: boiled with onion, garlic, and the local aromatic (either epazote or *hoja santa* or avocado leaves). In some places, pork and tomato are added to the beans (see Northern-Style Beans, page 66) and sometimes they are served with cheese on top, but in general, we like for the beans to shine.

In the north of Mexico, lighter colored beans, like pinto and flor de mayo, are the norm, whereas in the center and south of the country, black beans are much more common.

We are also very in touch with the lifecycle that beans have. We always make a big batch of beans and we know that they will evolve day by day. The first day, they are brothy and firm. The next day, the broth gets cloudier and the beans softer and so on until you have a homogenous paste later in the week. Then you start again with a fresh pot. This process is aided by the daily refrying of beans (typically with lard). Refrying comes from a time when there was no refrigeration and beans had to be refried every day to make sure they wouldn't spoil.

Basic
Beans

Preparation time
10 minutes
Cooking time
1½–2 hours
Makes
7–8 cups (1.6–1.9 liters)

2 cups dried beans, any kind,
   preferably heirloom
½ medium white onion, halved
5 large garlic cloves, peeled
½ cup avocado leaves, toasted;
   1 bunch fresh epazote; or
   5 hoja santa leaves (Mexican
   root beer leaves)
3 tablespoons salt, or more to
   taste

ⅱDF ℥GF ◖V ✦VEG ⌂5

As soon as children are old enough to help in the kitchen, one of the first tasks they will be asked to do is pick through the beans. Most of the beans in Mexico are still grown by small-scale farmers and therefore tend to have tiny pebbles or a twig, or just a couple of ugly beans. It is very important to pick through them. An easy way is to spread them on a table to sort.

A lot of households, especially more traditional ones, have a pot especially reserved for beans. It is made out of clay, is narrow at the neck, and widens again at the mouth, shaped like an hourglass. It is typically accompanied by a smaller clay pot or bowl with handles that is used as a lid. Fill that small pot with water, place it at the mouth of the large one (as a lid), and the water will heat up while the beans are cooking underneath it. It will stay hot so you can add more water to the cooking beans when they need it. We encourage you to try to cook them in a clay pot, but any large pot will do. Just make sure you have that extra hot water at hand.

———

Pick through the beans (see headnote) to remove any debris or imperfect beans. Place the beans in a colander and rinse under running water until the water runs clear. Place them in the pot and add loosely double their volume of water (a little more than 4 cups/ 945 ml/32 fl oz). You can soak them overnight at this stage—if they are very dry—and that will reduce the cooking time the next day or you can cook them right away. When soaking overnight, we like to use the soaking water to cook the beans so as not to lose its flavor.

Add the onion and garlic to the beans and bring to a boil over high heat. Boil for 5–10 minutes, then reduce to a simmer. If using avocado leaves, add them at this point. Cover the pot and cook for 1 hour, checking the beans every 10–15 minutes and adding more hot water if necessary. The beans should always be generously covered in liquid. (If you have a clay bean pot with the pot-as-a-lid, you will have hot water at the ready. If using a regular pot, keep a small pot of water over low heat on another burner for adding water to the beans if necessary.)

After 1 hour, pick out a bean and try it. If you can comfortably bite through it, but it still has bite, then it is almost done. If not, keep cooking until you get to that point. If using epazote or *hoja santa*, add them now. Add the salt (if salt is added any earlier, the skin on the beans gets tough). Continue to cook until the beans are creamy inside but hold their shape. Bean cooking times vary greatly depending on the hardness of the water, the freshness of the dried beans, the type of pot, and so on. So make sure you constantly taste the beans to determine their doneness. Serve fresh in a bowl or refrigerate in their liquid for up to 1 week or freeze for up to 2 months. Every time you reheat, refry the beans (see page 67).

Northern-Style Beans

Frijoles charros (frijoles puercos)

Preparation time
10 minutes
Cooking time
1½–2 hours
Serves 6–8

2½ cups (485 g) pale creamy preferably heirloom dried beans, such as pinto, rebosero, or flor de mayo
1 large white onion, roughly chopped
6 garlic cloves, peeled, half whole and half sliced
4 tablespoons lard
1 small pig's foot, or 2 lb (910 g) pork shoulder cut in large cubes
1 cup (180 g) coarsely chopped tomato
½ cup (20 g) coarsely chopped cilantro (coriander)
3 tablespoons salt, or to taste

For serving
5 small radishes, finely sliced
Fresh flour tortillas (page 28), or fresh corn tortillas (page 24), if preferred

iDF *GF

The two names in Spanish for this recipe tell us a lot about these beans. A *charro* is cowboy, making us think these beans were a one-pot meal eaten over a fire out in the country. *Puerco* refers to one of the main ingredients, pork. But it is also a play on words, since *puerco* can also mean "dirty." The translation to "dirty beans" comes from all the additional ingredients that are added to the recipe. You can add any pork products: pork shoulder, bacon, sausage, or even pigs' feet, like in this recipe.

———

Pick through the beans, removing any debris or imperfect beans. Rinse the beans in a colander under running water until the water runs clear. Place them in a pot and add double their volume of water (about 5 cups/1.2 liters/40 fl oz). You can soak them overnight at this stage and that will reduce the cooking time the next day or you can cook them right away. When soaking overnight, we like to use the soaking water to cook the beans so as not to lose its flavor.

Add half the onion and the whole garlic cloves. Bring to a boil over high heat, boil for 5–10 minutes, then bring down to a simmer. Cover the pot and cook for 1 hour, checking the beans every 10 minutes and adding more hot water if necessary. The beans should always be generously covered in liquid. (If you have a bean-cooking pot with the pot-as-a-lid, you will have hot water at the ready. If using a regular pot, keep a small pan of water over low heat on another burner for adding water to the beans if necessary.) After 1 hour, pick out a bean and try it. If you can comfortably bite through it, but it still has bite, then it is almost done. If not, keep cooking until you get to that point. If they are not ready, make sure you constantly taste the beans to determine their doneness.

Meanwhile, in a large pot, heat the lard over high heat until it shimmers. Add the rest of the onion, the sliced garlic, and the pig's foot or pork shoulder cubes. Cook the pork on all sides until brown, 10–15 minutes. Add the tomato and cilantro (coriander) and cook for 5 minutes.

When the beans are done, add them to the pot with the pork along with all their cooking liquid. Cook until some of the beans have broken down, about 45 minutes longer. Season with the salt.

To serve: Serve hot either as a side or in individual bowls with radishes and tortillas on the side. Store any leftovers in an airtight container for up to 1 week in the refrigerator and up to 1 month in the freezer.

Refried Beans

Frijoles refritos

Preparation time
5 minutes
Cooking time
20 minutes
Makes
5 cups

4 tablespoons lard or grapeseed
  oil
1 small white onion, finely
  chopped
½ cup herb used for cooking the
  beans
5 cups (1.2 liters/40 fl oz) Basic
  Beans (page 64)
Salt

ⅠDF ⅩGF ⓃV ♥VEG ❭30 ✿5

In a pot, heat the lard or oil over medium-high heat. Add the onion and cook until translucent, about 5 minutes (don't let it brown). Add the herb and stir until coated with oil, about 10 seconds. Increase the heat to high and add the beans. You should hear a heavy hissing sound. Cook for 10 minutes. For a thicker consistency, you can mash some or all of the beans in the pot. Season to taste with salt and serve. You can refrigerate in an airtight container for up to 1 week from the original cooking date of the beans or freeze for up to 2 months.

White Rice (p. 70), Green Rice (p. 70), Red Rice (p. 71)

Rice

After corn and wheat, rice is the most consumed grain in Mexico. The most prominent rice production areas are along the northern Sierra Madre flatlands. However, the rice from the state of Morelos, south of Mexico City, is considered to be the best in the country. It has a long grain similar to Carolina rice but with the lightness and starch content of a basmati or jasmine. Whenever we can't find Mexican rice abroad, we use one of these latter two.

In Mexico, plain rice is cooked much like a pilaf—with oil and aromatics—and it is the most common accompaniment to meals, especially stews, or is simply enjoyed on its own with some *crema* on top. So serve it with any soupy stews that the rice might help soak up, like the Stewed Pork and Purslane (page 174), Chicken Tinga (page 122), or the Mexican-Style Summer Squash (page 108).

Old matriarchs say that you cannot get married until you can make perfect rice. It is not a complicated dish, but depending on your pot and stove, you may get different results. Eventually, you will get specific about your own ratios the more you make the rice.

White Rice

Arroz blanco
Photo p. 68

Preparation time
5 minutes
Cooking time
20 minutes
Serves 4–6

2 cups (475 ml/16 fl oz) water or
    clear broth (if available, any
    kind)
4 tablespoons vegetable or
    grapeseed oil
½ large white onion, roughly
    chopped
2 large garlic cloves, peeled
1½ cups (300 g) Morelos rice (or
    substitute jasmine or basmati)
1 tablespoon salt, or to taste
1 sprig fresh cilantro (coriander)
1 serrano chile, whole

❚DF ✹GF ❀V ✿VEG ▶30

Place the water or broth in a small pot over medium heat and gently heat as you prepare the other ingredients.

In a large sauté pan with a lid, heat the oil over high heat. Add the onion, garlic, and rice. Stirring constantly with a wooden spoon, to prevent the rice from burning, cook until the rice turns a very light golden color and the grains don't lump together anymore, 5–10 minutes. Add the hot water or broth and the salt. The liquid should taste seasoned; add more salt if needed. Bring to a boil, then reduce the heat to a very slow simmer. Place the cilantro (coriander) sprig and serrano chile on top and cover the pot with the lid. Bring the rice to a boil again, reduce the heat to low, and cook, covered, until there is almost no liquid at the bottom of the pot, and the rice feels just past al dente, about 12 minutes. Cover again and remove from the heat. Leave covered for 10 minutes so the rice can finish steaming. Fluff the rice with a fork and serve immediately. You can remove the garlic cloves, Serrano, and the cilantro sprig before serving if desired, but some consider them a treat.

Green Rice

Arroz verde
Photo p. 68

Preparation time
10 minutes
Cooking time
15–20 minutes
Serves 4–6

2 poblano chiles, seeded,
    1 whole and 1 thinly sliced
½ cup (20 g) fresh cilantro
    (coriander) leaves
½ large white onion, roughly
    chopped
2 large garlic cloves, peeled
1½ cups (360 ml/12 fl oz) water
1 tablespoon salt, or to taste
4 tablespoons vegetable or
    grapeseed oil
1½ cups (300 g) Morelos rice (or
    substitute jasmine or basmati)

❚DF ✹GF ❀V ✿VEG ▶30

In a blender, combine the whole poblano, the cilantro (coriander) leaves, onion, garlic, water, and salt and puree. Strain through a fine-mesh sieve, and set aside.

In a large sauté pan with a lid, heat the oil over high heat. Add the rice and cook, stirring constantly with a wooden spoon, to prevent the rice from burning, until the rice turns a very light golden color and the grains don't lump together anymore, 5–10 minutes. Add the poblano liquid; it should heavily hiss when you do. Stir briefly while it comes to a boil, for about 30 seconds, incorporating everything together. The liquid should taste seasoned. Reduce the heat to low, add the sliced poblano, and cover. Cook for 10 minutes or until you can dig a round hole in the center of the pot and the water is gone and the rice feels just past al dente. Cover again and remove from the heat. Leave covered for 10 minutes so it finishes steaming. Fluff the rice with a fork and serve immediately.

Red Rice

Arroz rojo (arroz a la mexicana)
Photo p. 68

Preparation time
10 minutes
Cooking time
15–20 minutes
Serves 4–6

7 plum tomatoes, quartered
½ large white onion, roughly
  chopped
2 large garlic cloves, peeled
1 tablespoon salt, or to taste
1 cup (240 ml/8 fl oz) water
4 tablespoons vegetable or
  grapeseed oil
1½ cups (300 g) Morelos rice (or
  substitute jasmine or basmati)
1 cup (125 g) finely chopped
  carrot
1 cup (145 g) fresh peas
1 sprig fresh cilantro (coriander)
1 serrano chile, whole

⦁DF ✲GF ⬬V ✦VEG ◗30

In a blender, combine the tomatoes, onion, garlic, salt, and water. Strain through a fine-mesh sieve set over a bowl and press against the solids with a spoon and set aside.

In a large sauté pan with a lid, heat the oil over high heat. Add the rice and cook, stirring constantly with a wooden spoon, to prevent the rice from burning, until the rice turns a very light golden color and the grains don't lump together anymore, 5–10 minutes. Add the tomato liquid; it should heavily hiss when you do. Stir briefly while it comes to a boil, for about 30 seconds, incorporating everything together. The liquid should taste seasoned. Reduce the heat to low, add the carrot and peas along with the cilantro (coriander) stem and serrano, and cover. Cook for 10 minutes or until you can make a crater in the center of the pot and the water is gone and the rice feels just past al dente. Cover again and remove from the heat. Leave covered for 10 minutes so it finishes steaming. Fluff the rice with a fork and serve immediately.

Breakfast in Mexico is a serious affair. Other cultures eat a simple meal in the morning, but we go big and flavorful. We have people over for breakfast. We have fine-dining breakfast restaurants. There are vendors selling tamales, *atole*, *tlacoyos*, fruits, and juices outside every subway station and bus stop in every city. Chilaquiles are served at weddings in the wee hours of the morning for breakfast before the guests leave. Ask any Mexican what he or she would like to eat on a Sunday after a late night out and the unanimous response will be chilaquiles.

First, we love our fresh fruit: There is such an abundance of tropical fruit in the country that juices and cut fruit are always at a breakfast table. Second, breakfast dishes tend to be a combination of the same ingredients: eggs, masa, salsa, and beans. We just switch things around a bit, but the combinations are endless: Enchiladas, chilaquiles, tamales, huevos rancheros, *enfrijoladas* . . . etc. Third, hot beverages—coffee, *atole*, or chocolate—are always accompanied by *pan dulce*, or pastries and sweet breads. With endearing names like *besos* (kisses), *conchas* (shells), and *cuernos* (horns), the tradition of *pan dulce* is yet another example of our cultural mixings, dating back to the French influence we so happily adopted at the turn of last century. Prepare some salsas and ingredients the night before, invite over friends or family, and treat yourself and them to our most cherished meal of the day.

BREAKFAST

Preparation time
5 minutes
Cooking time
10 minutes, plus salsa
cooking time
Serves 4

🥛DF 🌾GF 🍀VEG ▶30

2 cups (475 ml/16 fl oz) Salsa
    Roja/Ranchera (page 50)
Oil, such as grapeseed,
    canola (rapeseed), or
    olive oil
8 tortillas
8 eggs
Salt
4 hoja santa leaves
    (optional)

Huevos Rancheros

Photo pp. 76–77

Huevos rancheros is the most ubiquitous Mexican breakfast dish. It is so simple—tortilla, egg, salsa—and yet so satisfying. Its name shows you how basic it is. *Ranchero,* which means rancher-style, tells us it was probably prepared out in the fields. Since a Mexican household always has some salsa available in the refrigerator or pantry, making these is fairly straightforward and quick. But even if you have to make a salsa from scratch, it is still a quick and pampering breakfast to leisurely enjoy during a weekend morning.

The tortillas are lightly poached in oil to soften them and to protect them from falling apart once they are covered with salsa.

You can use any type of salsa or use two different types of salsas, one for each egg. We call that *divorciados* (divorced). You can also add cheese, refried beans, or avocado. You could even make *huevos motuleños,* a classic dish in Yucatán that features an unusual combination of ingredients— plantains, ham, and peas in addition to the salsa. Here, we present a couple of variations, but ultimately you can prepare huevos rancheros as you wish.

———

In a small pot, bring the salsa to a boil over medium heat, then reduce to a simmer and keep warm.

In a nonstick pan, heat enough oil to generously cover the bottom of the pan. Adjust the heat to medium-low so the oil does not smoke but stays hot. Lightly poach the tortillas one at a time until softened, 3–5 seconds per side; if you cook them for too long, they will harden. Transfer to paper towels to drain. Blot if necessary.

In the same pan, fry 2 eggs (or more) over medium heat. Cook until the whites are set, about 2 minutes, or to your preferred doneness. Season to taste with salt. Plate the 2 eggs as described below and continue cooking the remaining eggs, adding more oil to the pan as necessary.

To serve, place 2 tortillas on each plate and top them with an hoja santa leaf (if using). Place the eggs on the tortillas and cover with the hot salsa. Repeat for each serving.

Variations

Huevos Rancheros with Bean Sauce *(Huevos rancheros con frijoles):* In a blender, puree 2 cups Refried Beans (page 67) until smooth, adding bean cooking liquid or water to loosen until you achieve the consistency of heavy cream. Follow the huevos rancheros recipe as directed, but top the eggs with the bean sauce instead of the salsa, and about ½ cup (60 g) crumbled queso fresco on top.

Huevos Rancheros with Salsa Verde *(Huevos rancheros con salsa verde):* Follow the huevos ranchero recipe as directed, but top the eggs with 2 cups (475 ml/16 fl oz) Cooked Salsa Verde (page 48) instead of the *salsa roja,* and garnish with about ½ cup (20 g) cilantro (coriander) leaves.

Huevos Rancheros with Poached Eggs *(Huevos rancheros pochados):* In any of the variations above, you can poach the eggs instead of frying.

In a small pot, bring about 2 qts (1.9 liters) water and 1 tablespoon white vinegar to a boil. Reduce to a gentle simmer. Crack an egg in a small glass bowl or cup, taking care to not break the yolk. With a wooden spoon, stir the water in the pot until you form a whirlpool. Remove the spoon from the water and drop the egg into the center of the whirlpool. Repeat with each egg, keeping track of which egg went in first. Your first time, you should do 1 egg at a time and once you get the hang of it, you can do more at a time. Cook for 3 minutes for a soft yolk or up to 5 minutes for a firm yolk. Remove with a slotted spoon, letting excess water drip off. Blot over a paper towel and place in a bowl, with or without the tortilla underneath, and cover with salsa.

Huevos Rancheros (pp. 74-75)

Preparation time
10 minutes
Cooking time
15 minutes
Serves 4

♨GF ♠VEG ▶30

For the totopos and salsa
1 cup (240 ml/8 fl oz)
  vegetable oil
1 lb (455 g) stale tortillas,
  cut into 6 wedges each
Salt
2 cups (475 ml/16 fl oz)
  Cooked Salsa Verde
  (page 48) or Salsa Roja/
  Ranchera (page 50)

For serving
½ cup (115 g) Mexican
  crema or crème fraîche
½ cup (60 g) crumbled
  queso fresco
1 small red onion, thinly
  sliced
½ cup cilantro (coriander)
  leaves

Chilaquiles
Chilaquiles

Chilaquiles are such a simple pleasure but oh, what a pleasure. This is one of the most loved dishes in Mexico. I have not met a single person in my life that does not love them. Like with many other things in our cuisine, everyone has a favorite version. For example, there are some people who prefer the *totopos* (chips) soggy, some who like them still crunchy (I'm one of the latter), some who like them with *salsa verde,* some with *roja,* and some *divorciados* (divorced): *salsa verde* on one side and *salsa roja* on the other. Some like them topped with a fried or scrambled egg and others with poached or grilled chicken... or both. But most people would agree that a Telera (page 114), the classic Mexican bread, is a great accompaniment to sop up the leftover salsa at the end. And that drinking a beer with a bowl of chilaquiles is the perfect way to have a weekend breakfast, especially after a long night.

————

Prepare the totopos and salsa: Measure out 2 tablespoons oil and set aside. In a small pot, heat the remaining oil over medium heat until hot but not smoking. Without crowding the pot, fry the tortilla wedges until crispy and golden brown, about 4 minutes. Transfer to paper towels to drain and sprinkle with salt.

In a separate pot, heat the reserved 2 tablespoons oil over medium heat. Add the salsa (it should hiss) and bring to a simmer. Keep hot until serving and add water if necessary to thin it. The consistency should be soupy.

To serve: Evenly divide the totopos among four bowls. Dividing evenly, ladle the salsa onto each. Add eggs or chicken, if using. Add a dollop of *crema* and sprinkle with the queso fresco, sliced onion, and cilantro (coriander) leaves.

Preparation time
5 minutes
Cooking time
10 minutes, plus bean
cooking time
Serves 4

GF VEG

2 cups Refried Beans
(page 67) plus 1 cup bean
cooking liquid (page 64)
½ cup (120 ml/4 fl oz)
vegetable oil
12 Fresh Tortillas (page 24)
⅔ cup (165 g) Requesón
(optional; recipe follows)
4 tablespoons roughly
chopped epazote leaves
(optional)
Salt (optional)

½ cup (115 g) Mexican
crema or crème fraîche
½ cup (60 g) crumbled
queso fresco
1 small red or white onion,
thinly sliced

Enfrijoladas
Enfrijoladas

Enfrijoladas is a typical breakfast dish, but also a common supper dish. It is very easy to make, especially if you already have beans and tortillas in the refrigerator. In that case, it should take you no time at all to whip up a delicious, comforting, and nutritious dish. This dish can be stuffed with *quelites* (greens), pulled chicken, or fresh cheese, and served with sliced avocado on top and a Telera bread (page 114) on the side.

———

In a blender, puree the beans until smooth, adding bean cooking liquid or water to loosen until you achieve the consistency of heavy cream. Transfer the bean puree to a small pot and heat over low heat to keep hot until serving time.

In a frying pan, heat the oil over medium heat. Cook the tortillas in the oil until soft, 2–3 seconds per side. Transfer to paper towels to drain.

If using the *requesón*, mix it together with the epazote and salt to taste. Place 3 tortillas on each plate and spoon 1 tablespoon of the *requesón* over each tortilla and fold in half like a quesadilla. Otherwise, just fold the tortillas in half. Ladle the beans on top. Drizzle with *crema* and top with queso fresco and onion.

See next page for Requesón sub-recipe →

Requesón

Requesón

Preparation time
5 minutes, plus 1 hour
resting time
Cooking time
15–20 minutes
Makes
2+ cups (495+ g)

1 qt (950 ml/2 pints) whole
   milk, preferably local
1 cup (240 ml/8 fl oz) buttermilk
Juice of 1 lemon (optional)

❦GF ♥VEG ☗5

Requesón is used in a variety of preparations, to fill Tlacoyos (page 40), inside a quesadilla (page 92), spread on toast, and in desserts. *Requesón* is an inexpensive fresh cheese that is typically a byproduct of cheese making—very similar to ricotta. The whey that is left over after making the curds for cheese is cooked again and drained. And this is where ricotta and *requesón* get their names: *ri-cotta* in Italian means re-cooked, *re-quesón* in Spanish means to re-cheese. This recipe is a simple way to emulate that process and make *requesón* at home.

In a medium heatproof bowl that will fit over a medium pot, combine the milk and buttermilk. In the pot bring enough water to a simmer, leaving 1 inch of clearance between the bowl and the pot. Place the bowl over the simmering water and cook, stirring occasionally to prevent the edges burning, until the mixture curdles, about 10 minutes.

Meanwhile, line a colander with a double layer of cheesecloth and set over a bowl.

Pour the curdled mixture into the lined colander and let drain for 1 hour. Don't press. Refrigerate the curds *(requesón)* in an airtight container for up to 3 days.

You can either discard the whey, use it to make more fresh cheese, or use it to make condensed "milk" (see recipe on page 196). Cover the bowl with cheesecloth and let rest in the refrigerator for at least 1 hour and up to 12 hours. Repeat the double-boiler process but add the lemon juice. You will get fewer curds this time but this is a true requesón, the second cooking. You can combine the two requesónes or keep them separate.

Preparation time

15 minutes, plus marinating
and curing time

Cooking time

10 minutes

Makes

3 cups, about 1.5 lbs (680 g)
fresh chorizo

ÐDF ✪GF

For the chorizo

8 guajillo chiles, seeded and
  deribbed
3 ancho chiles, seeded
  and deribbed
1 teaspoon cumin seeds
1 teaspoon coriander seeds
4 tablespoons sweet
  paprika
4–5-inch (10–12.5 cm)
  Mexican cinnamon
  (canela) stick
1 teaspoon black
  peppercorns

1 teaspoon dried Mexican
  oregano
2 dried bay leaves
1 large garlic clove, roughly
  chopped
½ large white onion,
  roughly chopped
⅓ cup (75 ml/2.5 fl oz)
  distilled white vinegar
1 tablespoon salt, or more
  to taste
1 lb (455 g) ground (minced)
  pork shoulder

For the potatoes

Grapeseed oil or lard, for
  cooking
½ cup peeled ½-inch pieces
  potatoes

Chorizo with Potatoes

Chorizo con papas

Unlike Spain's chorizo, which is a cured sausage that belongs on
a charcuterie plate, Mexican chorizo is a fresh sausage that has to
be cooked before consuming. The spices, vinegar, and salt act as
a preserving agent so it lasts longer in the refrigerator than the raw
meat would. Chorizo is cooked just like any other sausage, either
whole—on the grill (barbecue) for example—or most commonly,
broken apart. It is practical to have in your freezer. When in a rush,
you can always sautée some and add it to a salad, a sandwich, beans,
a dip, or eat with potatoes or scrambled eggs for breakfast.

———

Make the chorizo: Heat a frying pan over high heat. Toast the chiles
until fragrant, about 30 seconds per side. Set aside to cool. Add the
spices and toast, stirring constantly, until fragrant, 1–2 minutes. Set
aside to cool.

If you have a meat grinder or an attachment to a stand mixer,
use that. Otherwise, in a food processor, combine the chiles, toasted
spices, oregano, and bay leaves and pulse until finely ground. Add
the garlic, onion, white vinegar, and salt and pulse to combine. Add
the pork and pulse until the mixture is homogeneous. Store in an
airtight container and refrigerate for at least 5 days and up to 10 days.
You can also freeze for up to 1 month.

Make the potatoes: In a frying pan, heat the oil over high heat. Use
1 tablespoon oil for every ½ cup (120 ml/4 fl oz) chorizo and ½ cup
pieces of potatoes. Add the potatoes and cook until golden, about
3 minutes. Add the desired amount of the chorizo, breaking it up in
the pan, and cook until dark brick colored and crumbly, 5–8 minutes.
Lower the heat and cook the potatoes until tender, about 5 more
minutes. Add more or less oil depending on your preference.

Variation with scrambled eggs (*con huevos revueltos*): Skip the
potatoes and fry the chorizo as directed above until crumbly and
brick-colored. Add 2 scrambled eggs per ½ cup of chorizo. Enjoy
with fresh tortillas and salsa.

½ cup (50 g) black or white chia seeds

1 cup (240 ml/8 fl oz) water

1 cup (240 ml/8 fl oz) coconut milk or Coconut Smoothie (page 224)

1 teaspoon ground Mexican cinnamon

1 tablespoon maple syrup, or to taste

1 vanilla bean, split lengthwise

1 cup (100 g) assorted roasted nuts and dried berries (we used a mix of pink pine nuts, pecans, pepitas, cashews, cranberries, and raisins)

Chia Pudding

Chia con coco y nueces

Chia, a wonderful seed endemic to Mexico, has long been known for its powerful nutritious content. It is rich in omega-3s and full of minerals. Its name comes from Nahuatl for "oily," *chian*. It was used by the Tarahumara people as their energy-rich food and it is also wonderful for maintaining happy and healthy soil. It is typically consumed in Key lime *agua fresca,* but we love to see how it is gaining traction and is being used in different applications and cuisines. It has the power to soak up to twelve times its weight in water, so it has great uses in the kitchen, like this pudding. It is healthy, filling, and delicious. You can top with your choice of nuts or fruits, dried or fresh.

———

Place the chia seeds in a large bowl.

In a blender, combine the water, coconut milk, cinnamon, and maple syrup. Using a paring knife, scrape the vanilla seeds into the blender and add the pod to the bowl with the chia. Blend the coconut mixture until smooth and add to the chia bowl, whisking to combine. Refrigerate for 1 hour, whisking every 10 minutes or so, to prevent the chia from clumping. Remove the vanilla pod.

Serve topped with nuts and fruits, or keep refrigerated in an airtight container for up to 3 days.

Preparation time
10 minutes
Cooking time
20 minutes
Serves 4–6

♣VEG ▷30

3 cups (440 g) fresh sweet
   corn kernels
3 eggs
½ cup (120 ml/4 fl oz)
   condensed milk
1 stick (4 oz/115 g) unsalted
   butter, melted, plus more
   for cooking
2 cups (260 g) all-purpose
   (plain) flour, sifted
1 tablespoon baking powder
½ teaspoon salt
4 tablespoons water
4 tablespoons agave syrup

Corn Pancakes

Hotcakes de elote

This is a very simple take on classic pancakes but made with fresh corn. You can just top with some butter or even maple syrup, but we suggest using this agave syrup with corn kernels. It gives it a beautiful depth in texture. To emphasize that, we add the corn at different stages in the cooking of the syrup; some will be fully cooked, even a bit candied, and the others will still have a bite to them.

———

Measure out ½ cup (75 g) of the corn and set aside. In a blender, combine the remaining corn, eggs, condensed milk, and melted butter. Blend until very smooth.

In a large bowl, mix together the flour, baking powder, and salt. Add the wet ingredients to the flour mixture and stir to combine.

In a small pot, heat the water, agave syrup, and 4 tablespoons of the reserved corn over medium heat. Bring to a simmer and cook until the corn is tender, about 15 minutes. Add the remaining 4 tablespoons corn kernels and cook until the corn loses its raw bite, about 8 more minutes. Add a bit of water if the syrup gets too dry.

In a nonstick frying pan, heat about 1 teaspoon butter over medium heat. Ladle ½ cup (120 ml/4 fl oz) batter into the center of the pan to make a 5-inch (12.5 cm) pancake. Cook until the surface is covered in bubbles, about 3 minutes. Flip and cook until golden brown, about 2 minutes. Repeat with remaining batter, adding more butter as needed. Serve with the corn kernel and agave syrup.

Large, showstopper dishes are no doubt fantastic and they will always be. But what about the dishes that remind us of our mothers, or of when we came back home from an after-school activity, or when we were not feeling well, or that we ate with our family for Sunday supper? These dishes might not be showy, but they are equally delicious and have a special place in every home, definitely in ours. In cities, they are also the kinds of dishes you will find during the week for lunch at *fondas,* which are family-style restaurants that cater to office workers. Typically vegetable-laden, the home-style recipes in this chapter tend to be a wonderful balance between healthy and tasty. They are simple and comforting and perfect for a weeknight, or when you just want a comfortable and cozy dinner. Many of these dishes keep well for a few days. They can be prepared on the weekend and stored in the refrigerator to be enjoyed throughout the week. Most can be turned into more substantial meals when accompanied by beans and/or rice and simple tortillas. Feel free to adapt these recipes to your tastes and preferences, using seasonal and local vegetables to make them your own staple dishes. Once you've mastered your favorites, you can always scale them up and serve to a larger group.

WEEKDAY MEALS

Preparation time
5 minutes
Cooking time
5 minutes
Serves 1

⚕GF ✿VEG ☽30 ⏱5

3 Fresh Tortillas (page 24)
3 small handfuls pulled
   quesillo (Oaxaca string
   cheese)
6 epazote leaves (optional)
Salsa of your choice
   (optional; pages 46–58)

Quesadillas
Quesadillas

The quesadilla is the simplest of pleasures. The return on investment on the effort it takes to prepare a quesadilla is enormous. It cooks in 5 minutes and can satisfy the hungriest of palates. In Mexico, it is the classic and ubiquitous dish that you make for yourself at home when you don't feel like cooking an elaborate meal, but want a feast for yourself. In its simplest, unadorned form—just cheese in the tortilla— a quesadilla is as purely delicious as a margherita pizza, but with much less effort. Like the pizza, you can add other toppings and fillings to your liking. We have added some of the most common fillings below, but feel free to experiment by preparing others or even using leftovers.

———

Heat a comal or frying pan over medium-high heat. Heat the tortilla briefly, about 15 seconds on each side. Place the cheese and 2 epazote leaves (if using) on one side. Fold over. Cook until the cheese is melted. Enjoy hot on its own or with some salsa.

Variations
Quesadillas with Squash Blossoms (*Quesadillas con flor de calabaza*)
Add 2 or 3 clean raw squash blossoms per quesadilla for a delicate simple touch.

Quesadillas with Mushrooms (*Quesadillas con hongos*)
2 tablespoons vegetable oil; ¼ small white onion, diced; 2 sprigs fresh epazote; 1 cup (80 g) sliced mushrooms, cremini (chestnut) or any other variety

In a small pot, heat 2 tablespoons oil over high heat. Add ¼ small white diced onion and 2 sprigs fresh epazote and cook, stirring, until fragrant, about 2 minutes. Add 1 cup (80 g) sliced cremini mushrooms (or any other variety) and cook until the liquid has completely evaporated, about 10 minutes. Add 2 tablespoons cooked mushrooms to each quesadilla when adding the cheese.

Preparation time
20 minutes
Cooking time
about 1 hour
Serves
4 plus leftovers

ⱯDF ✵GF

2 lb (910 g) chicken (whole or in pieces)
3/4 large white onion, roughly chopped
7 garlic cloves, sliced
½ cup (100 g) dried chickpeas (optional), soaked for at least 1 hour
1 sprig fresh mint
3 small carrots, cut into medium dice
3 fingerling potatoes, cut into bite-size pieces

1 chayote squash, peeled and cut into bite-size pieces
2 small zucchini (courgettes), cut into bite-size pieces
1 tablespoon salt, or more to taste

For serving
¼ large white onion, finely chopped
3 serrano chiles, finely diced
½ cup (20 g) chopped cilantro (coriander)
1 avocado, cubed
Key lime wedges
Tortillas (page 24)

Chicken Soup
Consomé de pollo

Consomé or *caldo de pollo* is one of the recipes that most reminds any Mexican of home. On a normal day, it is a delicious, filling-but-light soup. When you are sick or under the weather, it can lift up your spirits like few foods can. You can use a whole chicken or just thighs and legs, but I always prefer using bone-in chicken as it adds much more flavor. Scale the recipe up or down based on your needs, but this dish makes great leftovers. Squeeze a bit of Key lime into your bowl for a touch of brightness.

———

In a large pot, combine the chicken, onion, garlic, chickpeas (if using), mint, and salt. Add water to cover by at least 1 inch (2.5 cm). Bring to a simmer over medium heat and cook until the chicken is fully cooked through, about 45 minutes. Transfer the chicken to a plate and let it cool enough to handle. Shred or pull the chicken meat off the bone and return the meat to the pot.

Add the carrots, potatoes, and chayote to the pot and cook until the carrots are tender, about 10 minutes. Add the zucchini (courgettes) and adjust salt. Cook until the zucchini is tender but still bright, 2–3 minutes. You can refrigerate for up to 5 days or freeze up to 1 month in an airtight container.

To serve: Top the soup with onion, serrano, cilantro (coriander), and avocado. Serve with Key lime wedges on the side for squeezing. Accompany with tortillas.

Vegetable and Ayocote Bean Soup

Sopa de verduras con ayocotes

Preparation time
20 minutes
Cooking time
1 hour
Serves 8–10

⏱DF ✦GF ✦V ✦VEG

For the soup

4 tablespoons extra virgin olive oil
2 large white onions, 1 sliced and 1 cut into quarters
6 large garlic cloves, 3 finely chopped and 3 whole
1 cup (195 g) dried ayocote beans (runner beans), white or scarlet
2 chayote squashes, peeled and cut into large dice
2 fingerling potatoes, cut into large dice
4 carrots, cut into thick rounds
1 cup (155 g) fresh white corn kernels
Salt
10 very ripe plum tomatoes, quartered
2 zucchini (courgettes), cut into thick rounds
1 cup sliced mushrooms, cremini (chestnut) or any other variety
1 large handful of green beans, halved
1 handful fresh parsley leaves, roughly chopped
2 handfuls fresh epazote leaves, roughly chopped

For serving

2 serrano chiles, finely chopped
1 handful fresh cilantro (coriander), chopped
½ red or white onion, finely chopped
Key lime wedges, for squeezing

Hearty vegetable soups are always connected to the hearth and the home. In Mexico, we add the homiest of our herbs—epazote—an earthy, bitter, funky herb that we associate with the home kitchen. You find epazote throughout our cuisine, from a leaf added to a quesadilla to a bunch pureed into a complex green mole. It is a leaf that comprises the mysticism of a Mexican market matriarch—who always has the best stand and selection of herbs—yet is found in every home. Ubiquitous and magical, it is the special touch that makes this soup different. I like to make a big batch of this soup and enjoy it over many days. Just store it in an airtight container in the fridge for up to 5 days. For a smaller batch, just halve the ingredients.

Make the soup: In a large pot, preferably clay, heat 3 tablespoons oil over medium heat. Cook the sliced onion and chopped garlic until translucent, about 5 minutes. Stir in the beans. Add water to equal double the volume of the beans (about 2 cups/475 ml/16 fl oz). Bring to a boil, then reduce to a simmer. Keep a small pot with hot water on the stove in case the beans need more liquid. They should be generously covered in liquid. Cook until the beans are tender enough to bite into, but before they are fully cooked and soft, about 40 minutes. Add the chayote, potatoes, carrots, and corn kernels and cook for 15 minutes. Season with salt.

In a blender, combine the tomatoes, remaining onion and garlic, and 1 cup cooking liquid from the pot and blend until smooth.

In a large pot or frying pan, heat the remaining 1 tablespoon oil over high heat. Strain the tomato mixture through a sieve into the pan, pressing with a spoon until the liquid has gone through. Cook until the tomato broth has turned a dark orange, about 7 minutes. Pour the broth into the bean and vegetable pot. Add the zucchini (courgettes), mushrooms, green beans, and herbs and cook for 10 minutes. Season with salt.

To serve: Place all the garnishes in a plate or bowl at the center of the table and let each person add them to the soup to taste.

Preparation time
15 minutes
Cooking time
10 minutes
Serves 4

✤GF ♣VEG ◗30

1 cup (240 ml/8 fl oz) whole
 milk
1 cup (240 ml/8 fl oz)
 stock or water
3 tablespoons butter
1 small white onion, sliced
2 small garlic cloves, sliced
2 zucchini (courgettes),
 roughly chopped
2 lb (910 g) squash
 blossoms, stems removed
½ cup (20 g) fresh epazote
 leaves (dried will also
 work)

1 teaspoon salt, or more to
 taste
4 tablespoons crumbled
 queso fresco, for serving

Cream of Squash Blossom Soup

Sopa de flor de calabaza

This soup is quite a treat. Whenever the rainy season starts in Mexico, at the beginning of the summer, you start seeing big bunches of squash blossoms adorning market stands. This is a very simple soup to make, but its flavors are so delicate. It is sort of an everyday delicacy. Be careful to not overcook the squash blossoms as they will start to get a little bitter and their bright flavor will disappear. You can serve the soup hot or at room temperature.

———

In a small pot, heat the milk and stock over medium-high heat. Reduce the heat to low and cover to keep hot.

In a medium pot, melt the butter over medium-high heat. Add the onion and garlic and cook until translucent, about 5 minutes. Add the zucchini (courgettes) and cook until bright green, about 3 minutes. Set aside 4–8 blossoms for garnish. Add the rest to the pot along with the epazote and stir until coated with butter and starting to wilt, 30–45 seconds. Add the stock/milk mixture along with the salt and bring to a boil. Remove from the heat and transfer to a blender. Blend until smooth. Strain through a fine-mesh sieve and serve immediately or cool to room temperature. Serve in bowls and garnish with a few blossoms or their petals, and sprinkle with queso fresco.

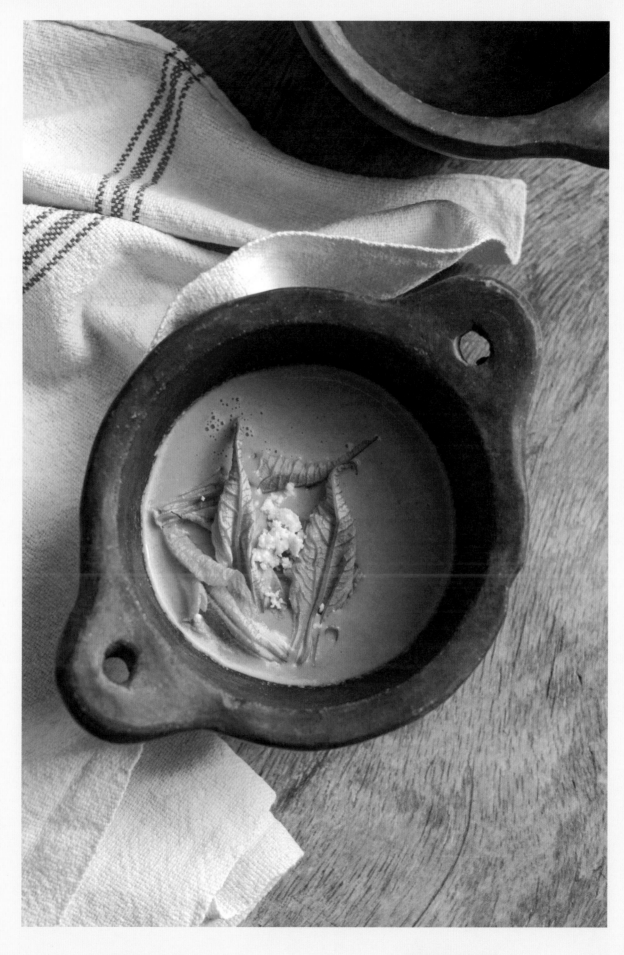

Preparation time
10 minutes
Cooking time
15–20 minutes, plus bean
    cooking time
Serves 4

GF ✿VEG

½ white onion
1 garlic clove, peeled
2 plum tomatoes, quartered
2 cups (475 ml/16 fl oz) Basic
    Beans (page 64), made
    with black beans
2 cups (475 ml/16 fl oz)
    cooking liquid from the
    same beans
3 tablespoons lard or
    grapeseed oil
Salt

Grapeseed or vegetable oil,
    for frying
4–5 stale corn tortillas, cut
    into squares or thin strips
½ cup (115 g) crema or
    crème fraîche
1 avocado, cut into cubes
1 chipotle chile, very thinly
    sliced

Bean Soup
Sopa de frijol

Cooked beans have a lifecycle of several days in Mexico: They are always made in a big batch and then used for 4 or 5 days. As they age, they are different in texture and flavor and therefore have different uses. However, bean soup is one of those ultimate leftover dishes that you can very quickly and easily prepare any day during the bean cycle. Depending on how thick or thin your beans are, or on your personal preference, you can adjust consistency by modifying the ratio of beans to their cooking liquid. The garnishes that we chose are typically used for their contrasting textures. However, a lot of people like using cubes of *queso panela*, a fresh and light cheese. You can modify the garnishes to your preference too. Needless to say, you can also substitute the type of beans used.

———

In a blender, combine the onion, garlic, and tomatoes and blend until smooth. Add half of the beans and half of the bean liquid and blend into a thin puree.

In a large pot, heat the lard or grapeseed oil over high heat until shimmering. Add the bean puree and the remaining beans and bean cooking liquid. Bring to a boil, then reduce to a simmer and cook until flavors meld, for 10 minutes. Season to taste with salt.

Meanwhile, in a small frying pan, heat enough grapeseed oil to coat the bottom over medium-high heat until shimmering. Add the tortilla pieces and fry until crispy, about 2 minutes. Transfer to paper towels to drain.

Serve individual portions of the soup topped with a dollop of *crema* followed by the tortilla strips, avocado, and chipotle to taste. (Alternatively, bring to the table in a serving bowl and place all garnishes in separate bowls or ramekins and let everyone customize their own soup.)

Preparation time
20 minutes
Cooking time
30 minutes
Serves 2–4

🥛DF ✲GF ◐V ✦VEG

¾ cup (145 g) dried lentils, rinsed and picked over
½ small white onion
3 small garlic cloves, peeled
Salt
2 pasilla mixe chiles, seeded (substitute with dry chipotle chiles)
1 cup (145 g) salted roasted peanuts
⅔ cup (150 ml/5 fl oz) extra virgin olive oil

½ cup finely chopped red onion
5 small tomatillos, husked, rinsed, and chopped into small cubes
½ cup (20 g) finely chopped fresh cilantro (coriander) stems (reserve the leaves for serving)
Key lime juice
1 small avocado, cubed
Tostadas (page 26)

Lentil Salad
Ensalada de lentejas

This is a great, filling, fresh dish that was inspired by ceviche. Instead of fish, it has lentils. It is important to very slightly undercook the lentils so they do not get mushy. Top the tostadas with lentil salad in the kitchen and serve right away, or serve the salad with the tostadas on the side and assemble at the table as you go.

———

In a pot, combine the lentils, white onion, garlic, and 1 teaspoon salt. Add enough water to cover the lentils by at least 2 inches. Cook over medium heat until the lentils are tender but not mushy, about 25 minutes. Remove the onion and garlic and discard. Adjust the salt to taste. Drain the lentils and set aside to cool to room temperature.

On a comal or frying pan over high heat, toast the pasilla mixe chiles on all sides until fragrant, 1–2 minutes, careful not to burn them. In a food processor, pulse half of the peanuts with the oil and the pasilla chiles until a thick paste is formed. Set aside.

In a bowl, combine the red onion, tomatillos, cilantro (coriander) stems, cooked lentils (at room temperature), and the remaining whole peanuts. Mix well with a wooden spoon. Slowly add the peanut/pasilla dressing. Season with Key lime juice and salt to taste. Add the avocado cubes and gently stir them in, top with cilantro leaves, and serve with small tostadas on the side.

Preparation time
10 minutes
Cooking time
15–20 minutes
Serves 4

⬗DF ⬗GF ⬗V ⬗VEG ⬗30

1 cup (180 g) white quinoa
1 cup (180 g) red quinoa
3 cups (710 ml/24 fl oz)
   water
Salt
1 small red onion, diced
3 plum tomatoes, diced
1 cup (20 g) cilantro
   (coriander) leaves
2 serrano chiles, seeded
   and diced (adjust quantity
   to taste)

4 tablespoons extra virgin
   olive oil
Juice of 2 Key limes
Tostadas (page 26),
   for serving

Quinoa Salad

Quinoa a la mexicana

Anything prepared with tomato, cilantro (coriander), onions, and serrano is *a la mexicana*. It is a very common preparation. This is a salad with quinoa, a crunchy and earthy grain, and the *mexicana* preparation, a bright counterpoint to the quinoa. Although it sounds very simple, it is one of my favorite salads—fresh but filling. The salad can be topped with sliced avocado or grilled chicken, or both. Enjoy it on its own or as a side.

———

In a wide saucepan, combine the two quinoas and toast over high heat for about 1 minute. Add the water and season with salt. Bring to a boil, then reduce the heat to low and cook uncovered, until the water has evaporated and the quinoa has bloomed, about 20 minutes. Let cool.

In a bowl, mix together the cooked quinoa, onion, tomatoes, cilantro (coriander), chiles, olive oil, and Key lime juice. Season to taste with salt and serve with tostadas on the side.

Preparation time
25 minutes
Cooking time
20 minutes
Serves 2–4

♣VEG

6 tender nopales (cactus
  paddles), spines scraped
  off
Salt
1 cup (240 ml/ 8 fl oz)
  Escabeche (page 60)
Juice of 2 Key limes, or to
  taste
3 tablespoons soy sauce
½ cup (10 g) cilantro
  (coriander) leaves
½ cup (40 g) purslane
  shoots, lettuce hearts, or
  other tender young greens
1 cup (120 g) crumbled
  Cotija cheese
Tostadas (page 26),
  for serving

Cactus Salad

Ensalada de nopal

Nopal—cactus paddles—are cheap and easy to find in Mexico and are full of nutrients and flavor. Look for the thinnest paddles for this salad as they are the most tender. *Nopal* salad can be made with either raw or cooked *nopales*. Here we chose to do both to increase the depth of flavor; and we also slice them as thinly as possible. If you don't have Escabeche (page 60) in your kitchen, or don't have time to make it, you can swap in chopped tomatoes and onions and some vinegar. If you can't find Cotija cheese, you can use half ricotta salata and half queso fresco mixed together, or omit it for a vegan dish.

———

In a frying pan over high heat, cook half the *nopales* until charred, about 8 minutes per side. When cool enough to handle, thinly slice. Reserve.

Meanwhile, thinly slice the remaining *nopales*. Place them in a colander, add a couple of generous sprinkles of salt, and vigorously toss using your hands. You will immediately see them exude slime. Let them rest for 10 minutes. Rinse under cold running water.

In a medium bowl, combine the charred and raw *nopales*, the escabeche, Key lime juice, and soy sauce and mix until incorporated. Add the cilantro (coriander) and purslane and toss once or twice more. Transfer to serving bowls. Sprinkle Cotija on top and serve tostadas on the side.

Preparation time
10 minutes
Cooking time
20 minutes
Serves 2–4

◉DF ✌GF ⦿V ✚VEG ▶30

2 tablespoons vegetable oil
½ large onion, cut into
   medium dice
3 small garlic cloves, sliced
1 cob fresh white corn,
   kernels
1 small serrano chile,
   seeded and finely
   chopped
1 lb (455 g) plum tomatoes,
   roughly chopped

1 lb (455 g) heirloom
   summer squash or
   zucchini (courgettes),
   thickly sliced
½ cup (10 g) fresh epazote
   leaves
Salt

Mexican-Style Summer Squash

Calabacitas a la mexicana

A la Mexicana—a preparation with tomatoes (red), onions (white), and serrano chiles (green)—gets its name from the colors of our flag. This is one of the most classic expressions of the *mexicana* style and a typical side dish at home. Every household has a version of it. It is easy, packed with flavor and nutrients, and perfectly satisfying. Serve with rice or on its own and change up the squashes based on the season.

In a large pot, heat the oil over medium heat. Add the onion, garlic, and corn kernels and cook until the onion is translucent, about 5 minutes. Add the serrano and tomatoes. Cook for another 5 minutes, until the tomatoes start changing color to a brick orange. Add the squash and the epazote. Cook until the tomatoes completely change color and start falling apart, for another 5–10 minutes. Season to taste with salt and serve hot.

Preparation time
15 minutes
Cooking time
30 minutes
Serves 4

DF GF

4 large squares (about
10 inches/25 cm) of
banana leaf
1 skinless sea bass fillet
(1½ lb/680 g)
Salt
1 Key lime, sliced
1 lemon, sliced
3–4 sprigs fresh epazote
3–4 sprigs fresh cilantro
(coriander)
3–4 sprigs fresh mint

3–4 sprigs fresh lamb's-
quarter, preferably small,
tender leaves
4 tablespoons extra virgin
olive oil

Baked Fish with Greens

Empapelado de pescado con hierbas y quelites

Beyond its use for tamales, banana leaf is a very versatile and commonly used wrapper. It is wonderful for holding in moisture, it imparts a unique earthy vegetal flavor, and it is beautiful to serve the dish in. On both coasts of Mexico, banana leaf is often used to steam or bake fish. For this recipe, instead of making a sauce or marinade, we decided to let the fish speak for itself, adding only some herbs and wild greens and some citrus for aroma. The quality of the fish matters a lot when steaming—we like to use a thicker cut of a not-so-oily meaty fish like sea bass. For the herbs, you can substitute whatever is growing in your herb garden or is available at the farmers' market. Serve with one of the raw salsas (pages 46 and 52) and tortillas (page 24) on the side.

———

Preheat the oven to 350°F (180°C/Gas Mark 4).

Hold the banana leaves 4 inches above an open flame until they begin to change color, about 1 minute. They should be a brighter green. If using an electric stove, heat up a large dry frying pan or griddle and press the leaves on the hot surface in quick intervals until they change color, just be careful not to brown them or dry them out.

Portion the bass into 4 pieces and season generously on all sides with salt. Portion half of the citrus and herbs onto the center of each banana leaf. Top with the fish, then top with remaining citrus and herbs. Drizzle with the olive oil. Wrap like a *tamal* (see page 34) and place on a baking sheet. Bake until the fish feels tender to touch, about 25 minutes. Serve immediately in its wrapper, letting each person unwrap their own.

For the fish
4 small (about 5 oz /150 g) skinless white fish fillets, such as sea bass or halibut
Salt and black pepper
½ cup (65 g) all-purpose (plain) flour
2 eggs
1 cup (115 g) breadcrumbs
1 cup (240 ml/8 fl oz) vegetable oil

For the tortas
4 Teleras (recipe follows)
1 stick (4 oz/115 g) butter, at room temperature
½ cup (110 g) Mayonnaise (page 120)
1 canned chipotle chiles in adobo sauce
4 large red leaf lettuce leaves

1 small red onion, thinly sliced
4 plum tomatoes, sliced
2 avocados, sliced
1 avocado, mashed
Salt
Escabeche (optional; page 60)

Fish Milanese Torta

Torta de milanesa de pescado

Tortas, the Mexican sandwiches, are a very common street food. But they are also the default food for picnics, road trips, sports games, and more. In Mexico, *teleras* and *bolillos* are the default *torta* breads. However, *bolillos* have a French crust and are therefore only good for one day. *Teleras* are much easier to bake and are more generous with time, lasting a couple of days. *Tortas de milanesa* tend to be with breaded chicken or beef, but I have always loved the texture of a fish *milanesa*, crispy and soft. For heat, we tend to add jalapeños in escabeche (page 60) to our *tortas*, but that is up to you. You can also prepare and serve the *milanesa* on its own or with some rice and avocado slices.

Cook the fish: Season the fish fillets with salt and pepper. Place the flour in a shallow bowl, beat the eggs in a separate shallow bowl, and the place the breadcrumbs in a third shallow bowl. Working with one at a time, dredge each fish fillet in the flour, then dip in the eggs, turning to coat and letting excess drip away. Dip in the breadcrumbs, turning to evenly coat.

In a frying pan, heat the oil over medium-high heat. Add the fish and fry until golden brown, about 2 minutes. Flip and cook on the other side until golden brown, about 2 minutes. Transfer to paper towels to drain.

Assemble the tortas: Slice each *telera* open horizontally. Rub the butter on all the cut sides. Heat a frying pan over medium heat and toast the bread until lightly browned on both sides, about 30 seconds per side.

In a blender or small food processor, blend the mayonnaise with the chipotle. Spread the chipotle mayonnaise on all cut sides of the bread. On the bottom half, place a lettuce leaf, some sliced onion, a breaded fish fillet, tomato slices, and avocado slices. Sprinkle with some salt. Place the top bread on.

Slice in half and serve with escabeche on the side.

See next page for Telera Bread sub-recipe →

Telera Bread
Telera

Preparation time
25 minutes, plus 1 hour rising
  time
Cooking time
20 minutes
Makes
12 teleras

1 tablespoon (12 g) instant yeast
1⅓ cups (315 ml/10.5 fl oz) warm
  water
4 cups (530 g) bread (strong
  white) flour
1 teaspoon salt
2.75 oz (78 g) fresh yeast

■DF ◐V ♦VEG ⚐5

Although great for *tortas*, we also like to serve *teleras* as a side to soupy dishes like Huevos Rancheros (page 74), since it's such a good bread for soaking up any leftover plate juices. It is also great just split in half and toasted and spread with some butter and jam.

———

Dissolve the instant yeast in ⅓ cup (75 ml/2.5 fl oz) of the warm water to activate. Set aside.

Combine the flour and salt on a work surface and make a well in the center. Slowly mix in the remaining 1 cup (240 ml/8 fl oz) water, the fresh yeast, and the hydrated yeast. Work the dough for 10 minutes until the mix is even and homogenous, adding a bit more water or flour if necessary. The dough should be tacky but not sticky. Transfer the dough to a bowl and cover with a damp cloth. Let the dough rise until doubled, about 1 hour.

Turn the dough out onto a lightly floured work surface. Divide the dough into 12 portions (about 80 grams each) and shape into balls. Using your hands, shape each ball into a ½-inch thick oval about 4 inches (10 cm) long. Place the rolls on a baking sheet. Use a dough scraper or a paring knife to score 2 parallel lines on the top of each roll, lengthwise. Cover with a damp tea towel. Alternatively, cover with plastic wrap (cling film) and refrigerate for up to one day or freeze for up to one month. Once they have doubled in size, about 30 minutes, they are ready to bake.

Preheat the oven to 350°F (180°C/Gas Mark 4).

Spray the dough balls with water and place the baking sheet in the oven and bake until the tops are golden brown, about 15 minutes.

Preparation time
35 minutes, plus
overnight soaking
Cooking time
40 minutes
Serves 4–6

🍴DF ✿GF

½ lb (225 g) salt cod, no
   bones or skin
4 tablespoons extra virgin
   olive oil
¾ cup (85 g) sliced white
   onion
2 garlic cloves, thinly sliced
10 very ripe plum tomatoes,
   roughly chopped
1 small bunch fresh parsley
   leaves, roughly chopped
½ lb (225 g) baby potatoes
   or fingerlings, cut into
   bite-size pieces

4 pickled banana peppers
1 red bell pepper, sliced
4 tablespoons pitted green
   olives
4 tablespoons capers or
   caper berries
4 bay leaves
2 lemons, sliced
½ cup blanched sliced
   (flaked) almonds
Salt

Veracruz-Style Cod

**Bacalao a la
veracruzana**

This dish represents what anthropologists call cultural syncretism: the union of two cultures into a fused reality. With ingredients from many cultures on both sides of the Atlantic and with a history that dates back centuries, bacalao a la *veracruzana* (or *a la vizcaina*) is a beloved classic dish for Christmas time. Our mother has made it for us since we can remember. I have now taken my mother's recipe, made it my own, and hope my children will do the same. The *veracruzana* sauce itself, minus the cod, is a great everyday sauce to have: It can be used over a simple fish fillet or grilled chicken cutlet. You can also stew chicken thighs in it. This dish also makes delicious leftovers—especially if the cod falls apart in the sauce. It is great the next day as a taco or on bread, as a torta (see Telera Bread on page 114).

To de-salt the cod, soak it in plenty of water for at least 12 hours, but for up to 2 days if possible, changing and discarding the water at least 3 times in the process.

    In a large pot, heat the oil over medium-high heat until shimmering. Add the onion and garlic and fry until starting to brown, about 10 minutes. Add the tomatoes and cook until they start to break down, about 10 minutes. Reduce to a simmer and add the cod and the rest of the ingredients. Cover and cook until the potatoes are cooked through, 20–30 minutes. Add water if the liquid is evaporating too quickly, it should be soupy. Taste for salt and adjust if necessary, though it probably won't need any because of the salt cod. Top with chopped parsley.

    Store any leftovers in an airtight container or zip-seal bag in the refrigerator for up to 1 week or the freezer for up to 2 months. Just add a bit of water to reheat.

Preparation time
10 minutes
Cooking time
35–45 minutes
Serves 4

▮DF ⦿GF

Fish a la Talla

Pescado a la talla

For the adobo
8 guajillo chiles, seeded
4 whole cloves
3 black peppercorns
1 tablespoon dried oregano
1 small white onion, halved
3 large garlic cloves, unpeeled
6 plum or heirloom tomatoes
2 tablespoons vegetable oil
1 tablespoon distilled white vinegar
Salt

For the fish
1 large skin-on red snapper, butterflied (or 2 skin-on fillets)
Oil, for rubbing
Salt and black pepper
Cilantro (coriander) leaves, for serving
Key lime wedges, for squeezing
Fresh Tortillas (page 24)
Salsa Verde (page 46), for serving

A la talla is a classic adobo, a spiced and saucy marinade, used by fishermen throughout the southern Pacific coast of Mexico. The fish is typically cooked over a fire directly on the beach. A great vegetarian option is a hearty squash such as acorn or butternut. Its earthy and sweet flavor is complemented by the tangy saltiness of this adobo.

———

Make the adobo: Heat a comal or frying pan over high heat. Toast the chiles, cloves, peppercorns, and oregano, stirring, until fragrant, 1–2 minutes. Transfer to a bowl. Put the onion, garlic, and tomatoes on the pan and char, about 10 minutes. Peel the garlic.

In a medium pot, heat the oil over medium-high heat. Add the toasted and charred ingredients and cook until tomatoes start getting mushy, 4–5 minutes. Add just enough water to cover the ingredients and simmer until saucy, about 10 minutes. Transfer to a blender and blend until smooth. Return the mixture to the pot and cook over medium heat, stirring until uniform and smooth, the consistency of ketchup, 5–10 minutes. Add the vinegar and season with salt. It should be on the salty side. Strain and let cool to room temperature. Use immediately or store in an airtight container in the refrigerator for up to 2 weeks or the freezer for up to 2 months.

Make the fish: Preheat a grill (barbecue) over high heat 30 minutes before you are ready to use. Rub the fish all over with oil and season with salt and pepper. Place in a grilling basket. Grill flesh side down for 1 minute. Remove from the grill, open the basket, and spread the adobo all over the flesh side, leaving the skin side clean. Return to the grill, skin side down. Grill, spreading the adobo every few minutes, until the fish is starting to flake or cooked to your desired doneness, 8–10 minutes. (You can bake the fish in a 350°F/180°C/Gas Mark 4 oven. Arrange skin side down on a greased baking sheet and spread adobo. Bake for 10–15 minutes. Spread more adobo on the fish as it starts to dry up, every 3–4 minutes.) Top the fish (skin side down) with cilantro (coriander) leaves and serve with the Key lime wedges, and tortillas, and salsa.

Preparation time
20 minutes
Cooking time
10 minutes
Serves 4

𝐃F 𝐆F ▶30

2 lb (910 g) very large (U10) head-on shrimp (prawns)
2 guajillo chiles, seeded
⅓ cup (75 ml/2.5 fl oz) extra virgin olive oil
Salt and black pepper
3 lemons, 1 whole and 2 halved and seeded
⅓ cup Mayonnaise (recipe follows)

Mayonnaise
1 egg yolk, at room temperature
½ teaspoon Dijon mustard
Salt
1 cup (240 ml/8 fl oz) vegetable oil, at room temperature
Juice of 2 Key limes

Salted Shrimp
Camarones con sal

The most important thing about this recipe is the quality of the shrimp (prawns). In Mexico we are lucky to have both coasts so close to each other, that the variety of seafood available in the capital city is outstanding. Go to a local fishmonger or market and ask for whatever the catch of the day is—prawns, shrimp, scampi, crab, etc. I prefer these on the grill (barbecue), but you can also make them in a hot frying pan. The best part about serving head-on shrimp is sucking the head juice when peeling them. It is the most flavorful part of the shrimp. You can eat them on their own or serve them with some rice (pages 70–71) and fried plantains.

———

Use a pair of scissors to cut through the shrimp (prawn) shell along the top and remove the vein.

Heat a small frying pan over high heat. Toast the guajillos until fragrant, about 1 minute on each side. Let cool to room temperature and finely grind in a spice grinder or food processor.

In a bowl, combine the shrimp, olive oil, and guajillo powder. Season with salt and black pepper.

Preheat a grill (barbecue) to high (or heat a frying pan or griddle over high heat). Cook the shrimp until evenly browned, 2–3 minutes per side.

Zest and juice one whole lemon. Add the zest and juice to the mayonnaise and stir to combine.

Grill (barbecue) the lemon halves cut sides down until charred (or char them on the frying pan).

Serve the shrimp with the mayonnaise and grilled lemons.

Mayonnaise
Mayonesa

Makes
2 cups (440 g)

In a bowl, whisk the egg yolk with the mustard and a pinch of salt. Whisking constantly, add the oil slowly, in a thin and steady stream. This will keep the mayonnaise from breaking. Whisk in the Key lime juice and salt to taste.

Preparation time
10 minutes
Cooking time
45 minutes
Serves 2–4

ⒹDF ⒼGF

1 lb (455 g) skinless,
  boneless chicken breast
2 large white onions,
  1 halved and 1 sliced
6 garlic cloves, 3 whole and
  3 sliced
1 tablespoon salt, plus more
  to taste
3 tablespoons vegetable oil
4 dried or canned chipotle
  chiles, chopped to a paste
9 plum tomatoes, roughly
  chopped

Chicken Tinga

Tinga de pollo

The first recipe any Mexican will cook as soon as they move out of their parents' home and live on their own is chicken *tinga*. It is easy, reminds everyone of home, and the ingredients are very accessible. Although it is better made with dried chipotle chiles, canned chipotles work if in a pinch. It can be a soupy stew served over White Rice (page 70) and with tortillas (page 24). If you cook it down to thicken a bit more, it is a great topping on a tostada (page 26) with fresh shredded lettuce, some *crema*, cheese, and fresh salsa.

———

In a medium pot, combine the chicken, onion halves, whole garlic cloves, and 1 tablespoon of the salt. Add water to cover and bring to simmer over medium-high heat. Simmer, uncovered, until the chicken is cooked through, 30–40 minutes, skimming occasionally to remove impurities. Remove the chicken from the broth and let rest until it is cool enough to handle. Using your hands, pull or shred the chicken and reserve. Strain and reserve the broth as well.

In a medium to large pot, heat the oil over medium heat. Add the sliced onion and garlic and cook until translucent, about 5 minutes. Add the reserved shredded chicken, the chipotle chiles, tomatoes, and 1 cup (240 ml/8 fl oz) of the chicken broth (reserve the rest for other preparations). Cook until the tomato breaks down and changes to a brick color, 5–10 minutes. Season to taste with salt. Add some more cooking broth if necessary; it should be a bit soupy. Serve hot or let cool and refrigerate for up to 1 week or freeze for up to 1 month in an airtight container.

Preparation time
20 minutes
Cooking time
30 minutes
Serves 4–6

☐DF ⚹GF ◐V ♥VEG

For the squash
6–8 zucchini (courgettes)
  or any variety of summer
  squashes, cut into wedges
Extra virgin olive oil, for
  drizzling
Salt and black pepper

For the mole
4 tablespoons grapeseed oil
1 small garlic clove, sliced
¼ small white onion,
  roughly chopped
1 poblano chile, sliced

1 fresh güero chile (or other
  yellow chile, such as
  banana pepper or New
  Mexico yellow), sliced
1 cup (150 g) finely diced
  tomatillos
⅔ cup (150 ml/5 fl oz) water
1 cup (125 g) roasted
  pistachios
1 cup (15 g) fresh cilantro
  (coriander) leaves
2 hoja santa leaves
½ cup baby spinach leaves
Salt

For serving
1 cup assorted greens, such
  as cilantro (coriander)
  leaves, cilantro blossoms,
  amaranth leaves, or
  purslane
2 cups (320 g) White Rice
  (page 70)
Fresh Tortillas (page 24)

Pistachio Green Mole

Mole verde de pistache

Mole comes from the Nahuatl word *mol-li,* which means salsa or sauce. Many think of mole poblano (or "the chocolate sauce") as the only kind of mole, but there are hundreds of moles that vary widely in style, for example, our very own mole recipe in Romeritos with Mole (page 164). Saying mole is like saying curry, it depends where you are, the local ingredients of that place, and the specific time of year. What all moles have in common is their celebratory connotation. There are moles made for the weekly family lunch, while others are for special events. For example, when someone gets married, the entire family comes together to make the mole days prior to the wedding. To illustrate how mole can be something other than a dark and mysterious sauce, we have included a fresh green version that is easy to make with seasonal produce.

Cook the squashes: Preheat the oven to 350°F (180°C/Gas Mark 4). Arrange the squashes on a baking sheet. Drizzle with the olive oil, season with salt and pepper, and roast until lightly browned, about 15 minutes.

Meanwhile, make the mole: In a medium pot, heat the grapeseed oil over medium heat. Add the garlic and onion and cook until translucent, about 5 minutes. Add the chiles and cook until soft, about 5 minutes. Add the tomatillos and cook until soft, 5–8 minutes. Add the water and the pistachios and simmer for 5 minutes. Remove from the heat and transfer to a blender along with the cilantro (coriander), *hoja santa,* and spinach. Blend until smooth, about 3 minutes. Season with salt to taste. Refrigerate leftover mole in an airtight container for up to 1 week. To reheat, add a bit of water and warm in a pot over medium heat.

To serve: Serve the mole warm with the roasted squashes and topped with the fresh greens. Serve with rice and tortillas.

Preparation time
10 minutes
Cooking time
30 minutes
Serves 2–4

⬤DF ✦GF ◑V ✦VEG

4 tablespoons vegetable oil
1 small white onion,
  roughly chopped
9 small garlic cloves,
  roughly chopped
8 dried yellow chilhuacle or
  6 guajillo chiles, seeded
4 plum tomatoes, roughly
  chopped
3 ears white corn
4 tomatillos, husked and
  rinsed

2 cups (6 oz/170 g) Brussels
  sprouts, halved
3 small hoja santa leaves
6 whole cloves, ground
6 allspice berries, ground
2 tablespoons sesame seeds
1 tablespoon dried Mexican
  oregano
1 tablespoon salt

Brussels Sprouts in Yellow Chilhuacle Mole

Amarillito con coles

Yellow *chilhuacle* is a rare chile from the Cuicatlán region of Oaxaca. It is almost exclusively used to prepare a mole called *amarillito,* which surprisingly is one of the simplest moles to make. Because of the chile's scarcity, most Oaxacan home cooks have learned to substitute guajillo for the *chihuacle*. Although the flavors are not as deep, it is still a simple and fresh mole and goes well with meat. We like to make this dish with vegetables (in this case Brussels sprouts) for a wonderful vegan version, but you could also add chicken or other proteins to this mole.

———

In a large pot, heat 2 tablespoons of the oil over medium heat. Add the onion, garlic, and chiles and cook until fragrant and translucent, about 5 minutes. Add the tomatoes and cook until they change to a brick color, about 10 minutes.

    In a separate pot of simmering water, cook the corn and tomatillos, for about 10 minutes. Scoop out of the simmering water and set aside to cool. Bring the water to a boil and add the Brussels sprouts to the same liquid and cook until bright green and crisp-tender, 3–5 minutes. Reserving the cooking liquid, drain the Brussels sprouts and set aside.

    Slice the kernels off the cobs and transfer to a blender along with the tomatillos. Pulse to roughly chop. Add the tomato/chile mixture, the *hoja santa* leaves, clove, allspice, sesame seeds, oregano, and salt. Blend the *amarillito* for 3 minutes. Strain.

    In a pot, heat the remaining 2 tablespoons oil over high heat. Once hot, add the *amarillito,* adding some of the Brussels/corn cooking liquid, if necessary, to achieve a thin puree consistency. Bring up to a simmer and cook until flavors meld, another 5 minutes.

    Just before serving, add the Brussels sprouts to the *amarillito* to reheat and serve hot in a bowl.

Mexicans have a gregarious culture. We love to socialize. We don't move around much, so our social circles tend to be tightly knit. Although this is changing, we are still a country of large families. For the generations that grew up in the latter part of the last century, it is common to have more than four siblings. A lot of my friends have more than twenty cousins whom they see regularly. It is not uncommon to get together with your high school friends at least a few times a month, even decades after you graduated. Celebrating a family event like a wedding, birthday, or graduation is always a large affair. Therefore as a culture we have developed a large repertoire of family-style dishes that feed a crowd. The dishes in this section vary in complexity, but they all have one thing in common: They are perfect to be shared. That said, you can still make them for a small group, or for yourself; just adjust the recipe.

A lot of these dishes are to be served directly out of the pot or a large vessel. Like the Pozole (page 158) or the Carnitas (page 176), guests serve themselves and finish their own dish with whatever garnishes in whatever amount they desire. Just lay out the plates or bowls, add some spoons and napkins, and bring out the big pot. Then your job as a cook is done—at least until dessert. Simply enjoy the company of your friends and family.

FOOD
FOR
SHARING

4 Hass avocados, at room temperature
1 serrano chile, sliced (seeded for less heat)
1 small white onion, finely diced
Juice of 1 Key lime
8 whole fresh mint leaves
8 whole fresh basil leaves
8 whole fresh tarragon leaves
15 whole fresh cilantro (coriander) leaves
1 teaspoon salt, or to taste

Herb Guacamole

Guacamole con hierbas

Guacamole is probably the most recognized dish from Mexico, and there are thousands of variations. We like adding fresh herbs for roundness and freshness, to contrast with the creaminess of the avocados. Beyond that, regardless of the recipe you use, there are two things that are crucial: First, use ripe avocados, they should give in to a light squeeze, but the flesh should not be bruised or blackened. Second, make sure your avocados are at room temperature. Avocados are mostly fat, and our palate can taste the nuanced flavors of fats when they are warmer. Think about it, what sounds more appetizing: warm butter on a roll or cold butter on a roll? It is one of the simplest pleasures of our cuisine. Enjoy with tostadas (page 26) on the side or as a condiment in tacos or other preparations.

———

In a bowl, mash the avocados with a fork. Mix in all the other ingredients until completely incorporated.

Preparation time
30 minutes, plus overnight drying
Cooking time
10–15 minutes
Makes
about 10 chicharrón sheets

❄DF ✿GF ⏱5

4 lb (1.8 kg) pork skin
½ lb (225 g) coarse salt, sea
    or kosher (flaked)
4 lb (1.8 kg) Pork Lard
    (recipe follows)

Pork Rind
Chicharrón

Eaten with salsa or guacamole, *chicharrón* is one of our favorite snacks. As a topping for a taco, it provides incomparable texture and flavor. It can be daunting to make, but if you are adventurous, this is a recipe for you. Although still great, store-bought chicharrones will never have the flavor of freshly fried ones. You can store leftovers in a closed plastic bag lined with paper towels in a cool dry place for 3–4 days. The chicharrones won't go bad, but they will lose their freshness. If this happens, make one of Mexico's favorite breakfast dishes, *chicharrón en salsa verde.* Just heat up a batch of Cooked Salsa Verde (page 49), add pieces of stale *chicharrón*—as many as will fit in the pot submerged in salsa—and serve with tortillas (page 24) and Basic Beans (page 64) or White Rice (page 70), or both.

———

Rinse the pork skin under cold running water. Cut into about 6-inch (15 cm) squares. On a baking pan, generously cover the skin with the salt on both sides and let rest for 5 minutes. Vigorously scrub the skin with the salt for about a minute or two on each side. This helps draw out excess moisture, remove impurities, and partially season the skin. Rinse under cold water to remove all the excess salt. Pat completely dry. With a sharp knife, score the entire fat side of the skin in 1-inch (2.5 cm) squares.

Dehydrate the skins for 12–24 hours (using the following methods 1 or 2), or until completely dry like hardened leather. The drier they are, the fluffier the chicharrones will be when frying. There are at least three ways to do this: 1) in a dehydrator; 2) in an oven set to 190°F (90°C); and 3) the traditional method, which is to hang the skins in the sun to dry for 2 days, wrapping them in paper towels during the night.

In a large pot, heat the lard over medium heat until very hot but not smoking. Fry the skin until it starts to puff, 8–10 minutes. Use two pairs of tongs, one in each hand, to unroll the skin as it fries, making sure it stays as flat as possible. When it is puffy, crispy, and golden, transfer to paper towels to drain. Cool to room temperature before eating or store (see headnote for instructions).

See next page for Pork Lard sub-recipe →

Pork Lard

Manteca y asiento

Preparation time
10 minutes
Cooking time
1–1 ½ hours

4 lb (1.8 kg) pork fat
4 cups (940 ml/32 fl oz) water

❗DF ✌GF ▶30 ⏱5

Lard is used a lot in Mexican cuisine. In recent years and because of health concerns, it has been replaced with "healthier" oils in many preparations, but there are some dishes in which the flavor of lard is necessary. For us, good-quality products are always good for you in moderation.

A byproduct of making lard is *asiento* (which literally translates to "that which settles"), and this sediment is incredibly full of flavor. We love to spread it on top of tostadas or *tlayudas* (page 26).

Lard has a shelf life similar to butter. It holds very well in an airtight container in the freezer for months. You can get pork fat almost anywhere pork is sold. Ask the butcher for a fatty cut such as jowl, belly, or back fat.

––––––

Very roughly cut the fat into cubes; the smaller the better. In a pot (copper if you have one), combine the fat and water and bring to a boil over low heat. Boil for 1 minute, then reduce to a very low simmer and let all the water evaporate, about 45 minutes.

Once all the water has evaporated, you will start to see the lard seep from the chunks of pork fat. At this point, stir regularly so that it does not stick too much. Once you have about 1 inch (2.5 cm) of lard accumulated at the bottom of the pan, keep at a low simmer, stirring occasionally until all the chunks are completely submerged in lard and have a dark golden color, about 45 minutes.

Remove from the heat and, using a slotted spoon, fish out all the chunks of fat. Strain the liquid through a fine-mesh sieve. The strained liquid is the lard. Let it cool to room temperature and use immediately or store (see headnote). The brown paste left in the strainer is *asiento*. Spread over a tostada with some queso fresco. Transfer it to a jar, let cool to room temperature, and store in the refrigerator for up to 1 month.

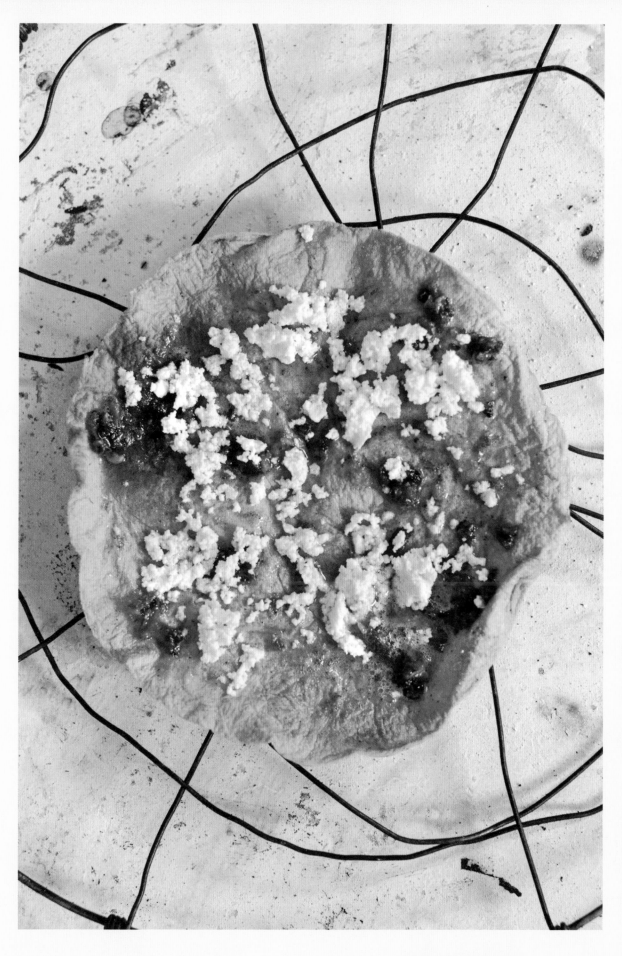

Preparation time
20 minutes, plus overnight soaking
Cooking time
3–4 minutes, plus bean cooking time
Makes
2 cups

ⅡDF ☺GF ◑V ♣VEG

2 cups (340 g) cooked ayocote beans (see page 64), plus 2 cups reserved cooking liquid
4 tablespoons Sesame Paste (recipe follows) or tahini
1 tablespoon salt, or to taste
4 tablespoons Key lime juice

For serving
Chili powder, for garnish
Extra virgin olive oil, for garnish
4 Tostadas (page 26)

Sesame Paste
1 heaping cup (150 g) sesame seeds
1 tablespoon cumin seeds
4 tablespoons extra virgin olive oil

White Bean Hummus

Hummus de ayocote blanco

Ayocote is a large bean we love because it holds its shape during cooking but is still soft and creamy. Just like its Middle Eastern cousin, you can use this hummus as a dip or add it to salads, wraps, or bowls. You can make a big batch (minus the Key lime juice) and keep it in the refrigerator for up to 4 days. The Key lime juice should be added at the last minute before serving.

———

In a food processor or blender, combine the beans, sesame paste, and salt. Blend until smooth and creamy, adding some bean cooking liquid if necessary. The consistency should be like hummus. If storing, refrigerate in an airtight container. If serving immediately, blend in the Key lime. Serve in a bowl, sprinkled with chili powder and olive oil, with tostadas on the side.

Sesame Paste

Pasta de ajonjolí

Preparation time
5 minutes
Cooking time
5 minutes
Makes
1 cup (200 g)

In a large frying pan, toast the sesame and cumin seeds over high heat, stirring constantly, until golden brown and fragrant, 3–4 minutes. Transfer to a food processor, add the olive oil, and pulse until smooth.

Preparation time
15 minutes
Cooking time
15 minutes
Makes
about 2 cups (475 ml/16 fl oz)

⬛DF ✋GF ◐V ✤VEG ☽30

2 guajillo chiles, seeded and
   deveined
1 cup (90 g) dried hibiscus
   flowers
1 cup (200 g) sugar
2 tablespoons salt
½ cup (80 g) tamarind pulp,
   no seeds
1 cup (240 ml/8 fl oz) orange
   juice
½ cup (120 ml/4 fl oz)
   distilled white vinegar
½ cup (120 ml/4 fl oz) Key
   lime juice

Chamoy
Chamoy

Chamoy is quite hard to describe. Originally, the word referred to
a type of pickled plum, much like Japanese umeboshi; but it has
come to mean any sweet, tangy, salty, and spicy sauce. It is a fairly
common flavor in Mexican candies, as a topping for fruit sorbets
or popsicles, and even in micheladas, the classic Mexican beer
cocktail. And it is a great accompaniment to both sweet and savory
things, like fresh fruit or potato chips (crisps). One of its classic uses,
though, is as a dip for crudités. Serve it with assorted cut-up seasonal
fruits and vegetables, such as cucumber, jícama, orange wedges, and
pineapple. and some spicy chili powder on the side. It is a perfect
daytime snack.

On a comal or frying pan over high heat, toast the guajillo chiles
on all sides until fragrant, 1–2 minutes. Let them cool to room
temperature. In a blender (make sure the jar is dry), combine the
hibiscus flowers, guajillo chiles, sugar, and salt and blend until you
form a powder.

Transfer the mixture to a small pot and add the tamarind pulp,
orange juice, and vinegar. Cook over medium heat until the sugar
dissolves, about 5 minutes. Simmer until the mixture reduces by half
and turns viscous, about 15 minutes. Strain through a fine-mesh
sieve and let cool to room temperature. Add the Key lime juice just
before serving. Store in an airtight container in the refrigerator for
up to one month.

Preparation time
10–15 minutes
Cooking time
35 minutes
Serves 6–8

GF VEG

For the esquites

3 tablespoons vegetable oil
½ white onion, finely
  chopped
1 serrano chile, left whole
3 large sprigs fresh epazote
2 cups (300 g) fresh white
  (or blue) corn kernels
3 cups (710 ml/24 fl oz)
  water
Salt

For serving

½ cup (110 g) Mayonnaise
  (page 120)
1 cup (115 g) queso fresco
1 tablespoon chili powder
8 (or more) Key lime
  wedges, for squeezing

Corn
Esquites

Esquites

No matter the size, Mexican towns and cities are designed around a central town square. Here you find not only the most important church in town or the government office, but you will always find a crowd. Whether they are using the central plaza as a meeting point or as a place for a lazy afternoon stroll, they will undoubtedly be snacking on something. One of these mainstay public snacks that is rarely found outside of plazas are *esquites* (stewed corn kernels). Most of the carts selling them will have a big pot with the cooked kernels and all the garnishes on the side—usually including store-bought mayo and chili powder, because they are both cheap and practical. No matter, because *esquites* are always satisfying and warming.

———

Make the esquites: In a large pot, preferably clay, heat the oil over medium heat. Add the onion, serrano chile, and epazote and cook until the onion is translucent, about 5 minutes.

Meanwhile, rinse the corn kernels in a colander under cold running water for about 30 seconds.

Add the corn to the pot along with the water and 1 tablespoon salt. Bring to a boil over high heat, reduce to a simmer, and cook uncovered until the corn is tender, about 30 minutes. Season to taste with salt.

To serve: Serve the *esquites* in individual bowls or cups with a dollop of mayonnaise, some queso fresco sprinkled on top, chile powder, and a squeeze of Key lime.

Preparation time
20 minutes
Cooking time
15–20 minutes
Serves 6–8

⬤DF ⬤GF

For the mussels
2 lb (910 g) fresh mussels

For the escabeche
4 tablespoons extra virgin olive oil
2 tablespoons grapeseed oil
1 small white onion, thinly sliced
1 garlic clove, sliced
1 teaspoon smoked paprika
1 serrano chile, sliced
1 very small habanero chile, minced (optional)
4 tablespoons distilled white vinegar
2 tablespoons rice vinegar
1 teaspoon salt

Mussels in Escabeche

Mejillones en escabeche

Escabeche is a style of pickling that, in addition to seasoning and enhancing flavors, is a great way to extend the shelf life of whatever you pickle. The smoked paprika in this escabeche does wonders for the mussels, really blending in with their natural earthiness. Also, feel free to adjust the spiciness to your taste. Serve this as a snack with toast or tostadas on the side, or use it as part of another dish.

———

Prepare the mussels: Rinse the mussels with cold water, removing any sand, debris, and beards. A brush might be helpful. In a steamer pot, steam them until their shells open, about 5 minutes. Let them cool and detach the mussel meats from the shells. Discard any that didn't open. Refrigerate until ready to use.

Make the escabeche: In a pot, heat the oils over medium-high heat until shimmering. Add the onion, garlic, paprika, serrano, and habanero (if using). Cook until fragrant, stirring constantly, about 1–2 minutes. Carefully add the vinegars and salt. Bring everything back to a simmer and remove from the heat. Let cool to room temperature.

Pour the cooled escabeche over the mussels. Serve immediately or refrigerate for up to 1 week in an airtight container. Let it come to room temperature before serving.

Preparation time
35 minutes
Cooking time
10 minutes plus octopus
   cooking time
Serves 6–8

DF

2 qts (1.9 liters) water
Salt
2 sprigs fresh epazote
1 ½ lb (680 g) large (U18)
   shrimp (prawns)
1 cup (270 g) ketchup
½ cup (120 ml/4 fl oz)
   orange juice
½ cup (120 ml) Key lime
   juice
1½ cups (25 g) cilantro
   (coriander) leaves
7 plum tomatoes, chopped

1 large white onion, finely
   diced
3 serrano chiles, diced,
   or to taste
1 octopus, tentacles only,
   cooked (recipe follows)
   and sliced
12 oysters, shucked
2 large avocados, cut into
   cubes
Tostadas (page 26), for
   serving
Saltine crackers, for serving

Cooked octopus
6 qts (5.7 liters) water
1 cup (130 g) coarse salt
10 bay leaves
10 black peppercorns
2 medium white onions,
   halved
1 head garlic, halved
1 octopus (3 lb/1.35 kg),
   clean and thawed

Seafood Cocktail
Vuelve a la vida

Vuelve a la vida literally translates to "come back to life," because it is typically consumed the morning after a late night out. It is spicy, salty, tangy, sweet, and has many different textures. It is truly reviving. I suggest you serve it for brunch. Do not worry about serving it with too much avocado or too many tostadas. Always accompany it with a cold beer or michelada, the default Mexican beer cocktail.

———

In a pot, combine the water and enough salt so the water tastes like the sea. Add the epazote and bring to a simmer. Poach the shrimp (prawns) until they are cooked but still tender, about 6 minutes. Reserving 1 cup of the cooking water, drain the shrimp and when cool enough to handle, peel and set aside.

   In a bowl, whisk together the ketchup, orange juice, Key lime juice, half of the cilantro (coriander), the tomatoes, onion, and serranos. Pour in some shrimp cooking liquid to lighten the texture if necessary.

   Add the cooked shrimp, the cooked octopus, and raw oysters. Garnish with the remaining cilantro leaves and the avocado cubes. Serve with tostadas and saltines on the side.

Cooked Octopus
Pulpo

Preparation time
5 minutes
Cooking time
1 hour

In a large pot, combine the water, salt, bay leaves, peppercorns, onions, and garlic. Bring the water to a boil. Once the water is boiling, take the octopus by the head and submerge into the pot three times before leaving it in the water. We call it "scaring" the octopus and it prevents it from toughening up. Cover and return to a boil. Reduce the heat to a simmer and cook for 45 minutes. Remove from the heat and let the octopus rest covered for 25 minutes. Use tongs to remove the octopus from the water and drain well. Remove the head and mandibles and discard.

For the fish

2 lb (910 g) fluke fillets

2 tablespoons salt

4 tablespoons extra virgin olive oil

For the salsa macha

4 tablespoons grapeseed oil

⅓ cup (80 g) finely chopped peeled fresh ginger

⅓ cup (50 g) sesame seeds

2 pasilla Mixe or chipotle chiles, roughly chopped

⅓ cup (75 ml/2.5 fl oz) fish sauce

⅔ cup (150 ml/5 fl oz) toasted sesame oil

For serving

½ cup (120 ml/4 fl oz) Key lime juice

2 scallions (spring onions), sliced

¼ bunch fresh cilantro (coriander), chopped

2 tablespoons crushed chicatana ants (optional)

Tostadas (page 26)

Key lime wedges

Raw Fluke with Salsa Macha

Crudo de lenguado con salsa macha

Although this dish has a decidedly Southeast Asian influence, raw fish in Mexico is always eaten with Key lime and chile. The dressing made with sesame seeds and oil is a take on *salsa macha,* a spicy oil-based salsa that includes a nut or seed with the chile. If you can't find the rarely seen but much appreciated pasilla Mixe chile, substitute with chipotle or morita chiles. We like to sprinkle chicatana ant powder on top because of its delicate earthy flavor. Unless you have recently visited Oaxaca, the ants will be a very tough find. You can leave them out or substitute with a light sprinkle of finely ground coffee beans.

_____

Prepare the fish: Cut the fluke into large cubes and transfer to a bowl. Season with the salt and refrigerate for 10 minutes. Coat the fish with the olive oil and transfer to a serving dish.

Meanwhile, prepare the salsa: In a small saucepan, heat the grapeseed oil over medium-high heat. Add the ginger and cook until light golden, about 2 minutes. Add the sesame seeds and cook until fragrant, about 2 minutes. Transfer to a bowl and set aside to cool.

Heat the same pan over high heat and add the Mixe chiles. Cook, stirring, until fragrant, about 1 minute. Don't let them burn. Add the fish sauce and cook until caramelized and thick, 1–2 minutes. Remove from the heat. Set aside to cool. Once cool, transfer the chile mixture to a blender or food processor and pulse until the chile is finely chopped. Add the sesame oil

Transfer the chile mixture to the bowl with the ginger/sesame mixture. You can make this ahead of time (it will last several days).

To serve: Add the Key lime juice to the salsa. Using a whisk or a fork, whisk everything together until just combined. Do not emulsify, this should be like a broken vinaigrette. Gently mix the scallions (spring onions) and cilantro (coriander) with the fish. Drizzle with the salsa. Do not toss or the fish might break apart. If desired, top with crushed chicatana ants. Serve with tostadas and Key lime wedges on the side.

Preparation time
25 minutes
Serves 4–6

⬤DF ✌GF ▶30

16 chocolate clams or any
  large clams
1 small cucumber, sliced or
  cubed
1 small red onion, thinly
  sliced
2 serrano chiles, seeded and
  finely diced
2 plum tomatoes, seeded
  and cut in small cubes
4 tablespoons extra virgin
  olive oil
Salt

2 avocados, halved
  lengthwise and then
  thinly sliced
10 Key limes, cut into
  wedges

Ensenada-Style "Chocolate" Clams

**Almeja chocolata
preparada**

The chocolate clam, which gets its name from the color of its shell
and not because of its flavor, is the largest on Mexico's west coast.
Because of its size and meatiness, it is much more pleasant to eat it
in small pieces, so for this recipe everything is chopped up, mixed,
and then returned to the clam shell. This style of preparing the clams
was popularized by La Guerrerense, a small food cart in the city of
Ensenada, and now, because of them, it is a staple of Baja cuisine.

———

Using a clam knife, open the clams and separate the meats from the
shells. Wash both the clams and shells under cold running water. Set
the shells aside.

Chop the clams into small pieces and transfer to a bowl. Add the
cucumber, onion, serrano, tomatoes, and olive oil. Season to taste
with salt.

Add 2 tablespoons of the mixture to each shell, top with
avocado slices, and serve with Key lime wedges on the side

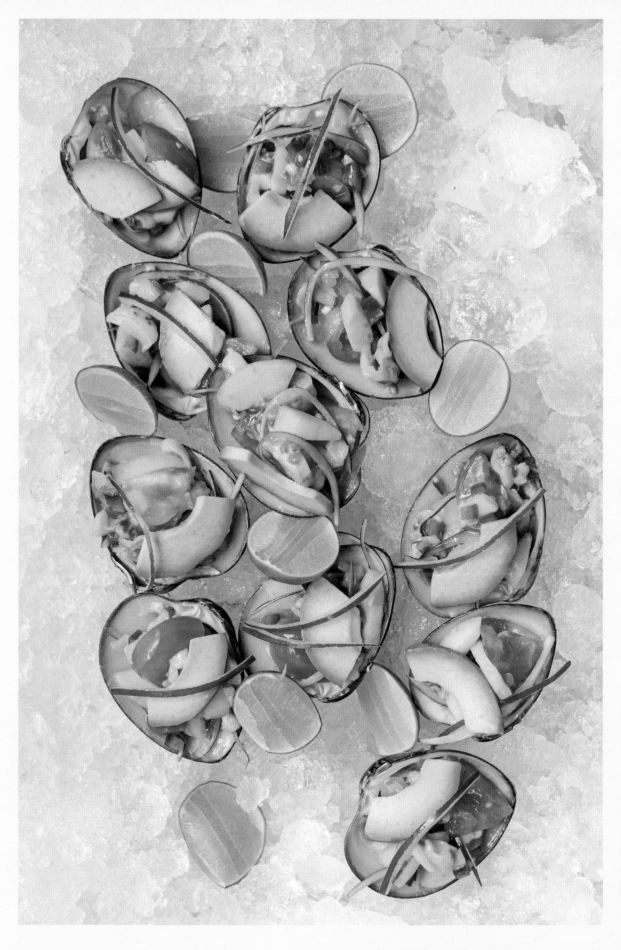

Preparation time
20 minutes
Serves 4–6

𝟏DF ▶30 ☗5

3 pasilla Mixe (pasilla
  oaxaqueño) or morita
  chiles, seeded
⅔ cup (150 ml/5 fl oz) soy
  sauce
⅓ cup (75 ml/2.5 fl oz) ponzu
4 tablespoons Key lime juice
2 sea bass fillets (about 12
  oz/340 g total), skinned

Sea Bass Sashimi with Mixe Ponzu

Tiradito de robalo y salsa ponzu con chile mixe

Tiraditos, or "throw-downs," are a take on Japanese sashimi influenced in great part by the prolific trade routes between the Asian Pacific coast and the Mexican coast. In Japan, the fish is thinly sliced for sashimi, but in *tiraditos,* it is usually also covered in a salty and spicy sauce. Because of this sauce, tiraditos are a richer alternative to eating raw fish in the form of sushi or sashimi. They can be made with a variety of fish, but what matters the most is to get the freshest fish possible.

———

On a comal or frying pan over high heat, toast the pasilla Mixe chiles until fragrant, 1–2 minutes, careful not to let them burn. Let them cool to room temperature. In a blender (make sure the jar is dry), blend the chiles to a fine powder. Add the soy sauce, ponzu, and Key lime juice and blend until completely incorporated.

With a very sharp knife, slice the fish thinly and arrange on a plate or platter with high sides. Right before serving, pour half of the sauce over the fish. Place the other half in a ramekin and serve on the side.

Preparation time
20–25 minutes
Cooking time
5–8 minutes
Serves 6–8

🍴DF 🌱GF

1 ear white corn
Salt
1–2 lb (455–910 g) hamachi fillets, or other oily white fish, skinned
3 small tomatillos, husked, rinsed, and cut into large chunks
1 small English (seedless) cucumber, cut into large chunks
2 small celery stalks, cut into large pieces

1 serrano chile, or to taste, stemmed
½ cup (20 g) chopped fresh cilantro (coriander) stems
4 tablespoons Key lime juice
1 avocado, cubed
½ small white onion, very thinly sliced
Tostadas (page 26), for serving

Hamachi and Corn Aguachile
Aguachile de hamachi y maíz

Aguachiles are originally from Mazatlán and the northern Pacific coast. *Aguachile* or "spicy water" (*agua* = water, *chile* = well, chile) is a watery sauce that you pour on top of raw seafood, especially shrimp (prawns), scallops, and occasionally fish. It tends to have four main ingredients: Key lime, fresh chile, cilantro (coriander), and cucumber and is served with sliced onions and sometimes more cucumber as a garnish. We added charred corn for depth and some celery and tomatillo for lightness and freshness, making the dish a bit more complex. The *aguachile* should be made as close to serving as possible. You can plate on one large platter down the center, or in two or three smaller separate plates, or even in individual portions. It all depends on the fish you get and how thinly you slice it.

In a small pot of boiling water, cook the corn for 10 minutes. When cool enough to handle, cut the kernels from the cob. In a dry frying pan, cook the kernels over high heat until charred, about 10 minutes. Sprinkle with some salt and set aside.

Thinly slice the hamachi and arrange on a large deep plate or a platter.

In a blender, combine the tomatillos, cucumber, celery, serrano, cilantro (coriander) stems, Key lime juice, and 1 teaspoon salt. Blend, then strain the liquid through a fine-mesh sieve set over a bowl (discard the solids). Adjust the salt to taste; it should be a bit salty. This liquid mixture is the *aguachile*.

Add enough *aguachile* to the plate or platter of fish to generously cover the fish. Add the charred corn kernels, avocado, and sliced onion. Serve with tostadas on the side.

Variation: Use the tentacles of 1 small octopus (see page 144 for cooking instructions) instead of fish. After making the *aguachile*, return the liquid to the blender and puree the charred corn kernels into it. It is a great way to add texture to the *aguachile* without losing freshness.

Preparation time
25 minutes
Cooking time
1 hour
Serves 6–8

ⅅF 🌱GF

¼ cup (60 ml) grapeseed or canola oil
½ lb (225 g) dried shrimp
1 lb (455 g) head-on small shrimp (prawns), peeled (reserve the heads and shells)
1 large white onion, halved
5 small garlic cloves, peeled
2 tablespoons dried Mexican oregano
10 guajillo chiles, seeded
2 dried Costeño chiles or chiles de árbol, seeded

8 plum tomatoes
1 large carrot, cut into small cubes
½ cup (75 g) fresh peas
½ cup (10 g) epazote leaves
Salt

For serving (optional)
½ cup finely chopped white onion
4 tablespoons minced fresh cilantro (coriander)
3 serrano chiles, diced
Key lime wedges
10 Tostadas (page 26)

Shrimp Broth

Caldo de camarón

Cantinas are traditional bars in Mexico where food is just as, or more, important as the beverages. *Caldo de camarón* is a classic cantina dish. Cantinas offer it two ways, broth on its own or with the vegetables and shrimp (prawn) meat in it. It should have a kick of spice that will warm you up and is usually served in *jarritos* or mugs. It is a great soup or appetizer to offer as a welcome beverage, especially if it is cold outside.

In a medium pot, heat the oil over high heat. Add the dried shrimp, shrimp (prawn) heads and shells, and half of the onion and garlic cloves. Cook until fragrant and the shells turn orange, 3–5 minutes. Add water to cover by at least 3 inches (7.5 cm) and boil for 30 minutes. Transfer to a blender jar and blend. Strain the mixture through a fine-mesh sieve into a pot (discard the solids). Set the pot of broth aside.

Heat a comal or frying pan over high heat. Toast the oregano and chiles until fragrant, 1–2 minutes. Set aside. Add the tomatoes and the remaining onion and garlic cloves to the pan and char, about 10 minutes. Transfer all the toasted and charred ingredients to a blender and blend, then strain into the shrimp broth.

Bring the broth to a simmer and add the carrot, peas, fresh shrimp (prawns), and epazote. Simmer until the carrots are tender, about 5 minutes. Add salt to taste, mindful that dried shrimp tends to be salty.

To serve: Ladle into bowls or mugs. Enjoy on its own or serve with the onion, cilantro (coriander), serranos, Key lime wedges, and tostadas on the side.

Preparation time
25–35 minutes
Cooking time
2 hours
Serves 10–14

⏳DF ⛌GF

For the salsa
10 ancho chiles, seeded
5 pasilla chiles, seeded
2 medium white onions
8 garlic cloves, peeled
3 lb (1.35 kg) tomatillos,
   husked and rinsed
½ tablespoon cumin seeds
½ tablespoon black
   peppercorns
5 whole cloves
3 tablespoons dried
   Mexican oregano
3 tablespoons dried thyme
Salt

For the stew
3 tablespoons vegetable oil
2 lb (910 g) prime rib of beef
Salt
2 ears corn, cut into 2-inch
   (5 cm) pieces
1 lb (455 g) fingerling
   potatoes, halved
1 lb (455 g) chayote squash,
   peeled and cubed
1 lb (455 g) carrots, thickly
   sliced
1lb (455 g) green beans, cut
   into thirds

1 lb (455 g) zucchini
   (courgettes), thickly sliced
⅓ cup (15 g) chopped fresh
   cilantro (coriander) leaves
⅓ cup (15 g) chopped fresh
   epazote leaves

For serving
Key lime wedges
Chopped fresh cilantro, to
   taste
Chopped white onion, to
   taste
2 serrano chiles, chopped
Fresh Tortillas (page 24)

Pot Mole

Mole de olla

Mole de olla is not technically a mole. Called *mole de olla* because
it is thickened and flavored with salsa, the dish exists somewhere
between a hearty soup and a light stew. It is a classic dish to prepare
when a lot of people are coming over for an informal lunch or
gathering. You could also make it for just yourself and refrigerate or
freeze the leftovers. Either way, *Mole de olla* is a wholesome one-pot
meal, and even though it feels indulgent, it's quite healthy.

———

Make the salsa sauce: In a frying pan or comal, toast the chiles over
high heat until fragrant, about 40 seconds per side. Transfer chiles to
a small bowl, cover with hot tap water, and let soak.

Slice the onions in half and add two of the halves, the garlic
and all the tomatillos to the same pan. Cook until evenly charred on
all sides, 10–15 minutes. Once charred, add the spices and herbs and
cook until the spices are fragrant, about 2 more minutes. Transfer
to a blender along with the drained chiles and 1 tablespoon salt and
blend until smooth. Strain through a fine-mesh sieve (discard the
solids) and set aside.

Make the stew: In a large pot, heat the oil over high heat. Once
hot, add the beef and the remaining onion and garlic. Season with 1
tablespoon salt and cook on all sides until browned, about 5 minutes.
Generously cover with water by at least 4 inches and cook at a high
simmer for about 1 hour, until the meat starts losing its tightness,
but still needs about 30 more minutes to get to fork-tender.

At this point, add the corn, potatoes, chayote, and carrots.
Cook until the vegetables are firm-tender, about 15 minutes. Add
the green beans, zucchini (courgettes), cilantro (coriander), epazote,
and the reserved sauce. Cook for an additional 10 minutes or until
the vegetables are fully cooked and soft and the meat is fork-tender.
Adjust the salt. It should be soupy and eaten in a bowl with a spoon.

To serve: Ladle into bowls and serve with Key lime wedges, cilantro
(coriander), onion, and serranos, and tortillas on the side.

Preparation time
30 minutes
Cooking time
2–3 hours
Serves: 15–20

🥛DF 🌾GF

For the pozole

1 bone-in pork shoulder
  (4–5 lb/1.8–2.25 kg)
2 large white onion, halved
12 garlic cloves, peeled
8 bay leaves
5 sprigs fresh thyme
4 tablespoons salt, plus
  more to taste
2 lb (910 g) nixtamalized
  white or yellow corn (see
  page 22)
10 guajillo chiles, seeded

8 ancho chiles, seeded
3 chiles de árbol, seeded
15 black peppercorns
1 tablespoon cumin seeds
4 tablespoons dried
  Mexican oregano
4 tablespoons vegetable oil

For serving

8 radishes, thinly sliced
½ head Bibb (round) lettuce
  or green cabbage, thinly
  sliced
20 (or more) Tostadas
  (page 26)
Árbol and guajillo chile
  powder
Dried Mexican oregano
Key Lime wedges

Pozole

Pozole

Pozole is filling, hearty, and perfect for a large group. For example, our opening General Manager, Gonzalo Goût, at our restaurant Cosme, used to make his grandmother's pozole for the entire team of seventy-plus every couple of months. You can scale this recipe up or down to your needs. Eat with tostadas on the side.

———

Make the pozole: In a large pot, combine the pork, half the onion, half the garlic, the bay leaves, thyme, and salt. Add water to cover by at least 4 inches (10 cm). Bring to boil and cook for 3 minutes. Reduce to a simmer and cook uncovered until the meat falls off the bone, about 2 hours. Add more water if necessary through the cooking process to keep the meat generously covered, and skim the surface of impurities. Strain the broth and reserve. Shred the meat and set aside. Discard the aromatics.

In a medium pot, combine the corn with water to cover by 2 inches (5 cm) and boil until it blooms like popcorn, about 1 hour. Add more water if necessary through the cooking process. Reserve.

Heat a frying pan or comal over high heat. Add the chiles and toast until aromatic, about 20 seconds per side. Transfer to a small bowl and cover with hot tap water to soak. Add the peppercorns, cumin seeds, and oregano to the pan and toast until fragrant, 1–2 minutes. Transfer to a blender. Place the remaining onion and garlic cloves on the pan and cook until charred, about 15 minutes. Add the charred onion, garlic, and chiles to the blender. Blend to a puree using chile soaking water to thin if necessary. It should be watery.

In a large pot, heat the oil over high heat and strain in the sauce. Stir until it turns orange, about 5 minutes. Add the pork broth. Add the corn and its cooking liquid and bring to a boil. Boil until the flavors meld, about 10 minutes. Adjust the salt if necessary. Return the meat to the pot and cook for 2 minutes.

To serve: Place the pot of pozole and all the garnishes, in separate bowls, on the table. Let every person add their own garnishes.

Preparation time
45 minutes, plus 2 hours
resting time
Cooking time
1 hour 30 minutes
Makes
10–15 tamales

GF ♦VEG

4 tablespoons grapeseed oil
1 small white onion, finely
  diced
2 small garlic cloves, sliced
2 small serrano chiles, finely
  chopped
1 small head of broccoli,
  florets and stems divided
4 tablespoons chopped
  epazote leaves
4 tablespoons chopped
  cilantro (coriander) leaves
⅔ cup (135 g) lard or butter,
  at room temperature

1 lb (455 g) freshly ground
  white masa (page 22)
⅔ cup (150 ml/5 fl oz) water
1 tablespoon salt, or more
  to taste
½ teaspoon baking powder
½ teaspoon baking soda
  (bicarbonate of soda)
10–15 banana leaf squares,
  ready for tamales
  (see page 34)
Broccoli Cream (recipe
  follows)

Broccoli Cream
2 tablespoons (30 g) butter
½ small white onion, finely
  chopped
1 garlic clove, sliced
⅔ cup broccoli florets
1 cup baby spinach
½ cup (10 g) hoja santa leaves
1 serrano chile, seeded
½ cup (120 ml/4 fl oz) heavy
  (whipping) cream
½ cup (115 g) crème fraîche,
  well chilled
Salt

Broccoli Tamales
Tamales de brócoli

Steaming vegetables inside a *tamal* is one of the best ways to cook them because their flavor gets trapped in the masa. Broccoli holds its bite, giving the *tamal* some texture. You could add any variety of salsa or cheese inside, or nothing at all, though this broccoli cream sauce really livens up the *tamal*.

———

In a medium pot, heat the oil over medium heat. Add the onion and garlic and cook until translucent, about 5 minutes. Add the serranos and broccoli florets and stems and cook for 1 minute. Remove from the heat. Stir in the epazote and cilantro (coriander) and set aside.

In a mixer with the paddle attachment, cream the lard or butter. Add the masa little by little until incorporated. Add the water and mix until incorporated. Add the salt, baking powder, and baking soda (bicarbonate of soda). Add the broccoli mixture and stir until incorporated.

Portion about 5 tablespoons of the masa mixture onto each banana leaf, fold, and place in a steamer. (For instructions on forming and stacking tamales, see pages 36–38.) Steam for 1 hour 15 minutes. Let rest for at least 2 hours. To serve, reheat in the steamer and pour some broccoli cream over each opened *tamal*.

Variation: Instead of broccoli in the main recipe, use an equal amount of purslane. Top with Raw Salsa Verde (page 46) instead of the broccoli cream.

Broccoli Cream
Crema de brócoli

In a small pot, melt the butter over medium heat. Add the onion and garlic and cook until translucent, about 5 minutes. Add the broccoli, spinach, *hoja santa,* and serrano and cook for 1 minute. Add the cream and bring to a boil. Remove from the heat and let sit for 2–3 minutes. Transfer to a blender. Blend on high speed for 2 minutes and transfer to a bowl. With a spatula or wooden spoon, incorporate the crème fraîche and cool the sauce to room temperature. Season with salt.

Preparation time
15 minutes
Cooking time
about 25 minutes
Serves 4–6

♦DF ✿GF ♦VEG

2 qts (1.9 liters) water
4 tablespoons salt, plus
    more to taste
8 fingerling potatoes, cut
    into wedges
1 sweet potato, peeled and
    cut into wedges
1 purple sweet potato,
    peeled and cut into
    wedges
1 yuca (cassava) root,
    peeled, cored, and cut
    into wedges

½ cup Chorizo (page 84),
    cooked
½ cup (120 ml/4 fl oz)
    Mayonnaise (page 120)
Vegetable oil, for deep-
    frying

Root Vegetables with Chorizo Mayonnaise

Tubérculos con mayonesa de chorizo

Potatoes and chorizo are a classic combination used as a side dish (see page 84) or stuffing for tacos, quesadillas, and *pambazos,* a classic street snack. This recipe has several root vegetables and uses the chorizo as a dip. There are hundreds of varieties of potatoes in the world, so you can swap root vegetables based on seasonal or local availability.

———

In a large pot, bring the water to a boil and dissolve the 4 tablespoons salt. Adding them separately, cook the vegetables until tender: fingerling potatoes and sweet potatoes for about 10 minutes, yuca (cassava) about 15 minutes. Drain, pat dry, and set aside.

In a food processor, pulse the chorizo until a paste is formed. Gently incorporate the mayonnaise with a couple more pulses. Set aside.

Pour 3–4 inches (8–10 cm) oil into a medium, deep pot and heat over medium-high heat until the temperature reaches 360°F (180°C). Working in batches, fry the root vegetables until golden brown on all sides, about 4 minutes. Transfer to paper towels to drain. Season with some salt and serve with the chorizo mayonnaise on the side.

Preparation time
45 minutes
Cooking time
25 minutes
Serves 10–12

❄DF ✢GF

For the mole
4 chilhuacle rojo chiles
  (or half anchos and half
  pasillas), seeded
4 chilhuacle negro chiles
  (or mulatos), seeded
4 chilhuacle amarillo chiles
  (or guajillos) seeded
1 whole clove
1 allspice berry
1 star anise
1 small (2-inch) stick of
  Mexican cinnamon
¼ teaspoon ground nutmeg
1 sprig fresh thyme
1 sprig fresh marjoram
1 sprig fresh oregano

1 tablespoon ground ginger
3 tablespoons stone-ground
  chocolate
2 tablespoons white sesame
  seeds
2 tablespoons roasted
  peanuts
2 tablespoons whole
  almonds
2 tablespoons pecans
2 heirloom tomatoes
½ white onion
¼ ripe plantain, peeled
2 large garlic cloves, peeled
2 prunes
1 tablespoon raisins
3 tablespoons grapeseed oil

1 cup (240 ml/8 fl oz) water
  or chicken stock
3 tablespoons kosher
  (flaked) salt

For the romeritos
½ lb (225 g) small dried
  shrimp
Salt
2 lb (910 g) romeritos
  (seepweed)
½ lb (225 g) fingerling
  potatoes, cut into bite-
  size chunks
3 fresh nopales (cactus
  paddles), cut into squares

Romeritos with Mole

Romeritos con mole
Photo p. 166

Romeritos or seepweed is a type of *quelite,* or foraged green, that used to grow wild in the fields in the late fall and winter months. It is now mainly cultivated since it is widely consumed in Mexico in December as one of our traditional Christmas dishes. It is very rich in nutrients and therefore also sometimes consumed around Lent, when meat is not eaten. It has a bit of a sour, almost citrusy flavor and has the texture of cooked purslane. It is called *romerito,* or little rosemary, because it looks like a rosemary plant, although the two are not related at all, either botanically or flavorwise. The typical preparation includes *nopales,* potatoes, and dried shrimp and is served with tortillas on the side.

The most important component of this dish, though, is the mole. Every family has their own mole or a regional variety. We like to make this Oaxacan-inspired recipe that we created several years ago for a friend's celebration. It has now become our house mole. If you don't want to make the mole from scratch (there are lots of ingredients!), you can substitute with a good-quality mole paste (see Note).

Make the mole: Preheat the oven to 450°F (230°C/Gas Mark 8).

Place all the ingredients except the oil, water, and salt in a roasting pan and roast for 8–10 minutes, checking to see that they do not burn. Remove from the oven and finely grind in a food processor until smooth.

In a large pan, heat the oil over medium heat. Add the ground mixture and cook, stirring frequently, until fragrant, 1–2 minutes. Add the water or stock, and the salt and cook, stirring frequently, until the mole acquires a homogenous color and texture and is reduced by a third, about 25 minutes. Strain through a fine-mesh sieve and season the sauce to taste with salt.

Make the romeritos: Place the shrimp in a small pot with enough water to cover. Bring to a boil and cook for 2–3 minutes. Drain and reserve the broth and the shrimp.

Bring a large pot of water to a boil over high heat and generously salt (it should taste like the sea). While the water is coming to a boil, clean the *romeritos* by removing the roots and any thick branches. When the water is boiling, add the *romeritos* and cook until bright green, 8–10 minutes. Remove from the water and transfer to a plate or bowl. Add the potatoes to the same pot and cook in boiling water until crisp-tender, about 2 minutes. Transfer to the plate with *romeritos*. Cook the nopales in the same pot for about 2 minutes, stirring constantly to help them lose excess slime. Drain and set aside.

Place the mole in a large pot and bring to a simmer over medium heat. Thin with a little shrimp cooking broth or water until the mole is the consistency of a runny puree. Add all of the cooked ingredients, including the shrimp and cook until the potatoes are tender, about 5 more minutes. Serve hot directly in the clay pot.

Note: You can substitute this mole recipe with 1 lb (454 g) good quality mole paste. Add it to a large pot, preferably clay, over high heat, and cook until fragrant, 1–2 minutes. Thin with a little shrimp cooking water, chicken broth, or water to achieve the consistency of a runny puree.

Romeritos with Mole (pp. 164-165)

Stuffed Chiles (pp. 168-169)

Preparation time
35 minutes
Cooking time
10–15 minutes, plus salsa
prep time
Serves 6–8

⏥DF ⌇GF ◔V ✦VEG ⏏5

For the chiles (*choose one*)
2 lb (910 g) fresh chiles, such as poblano, chile de agua, or jalapeño
or
1 lb (455 g) dried chiles, such as ancho, pasilla Mixe, chihuacle, or morita

For the stuffing (*choose one or mix and match*)
1 lb (455 g) quesillo (Oaxaca string cheese), pulled
or
1 lb (45 g) queso fresco, epazote leaves, and squash blossom petals
or
1 lb (455 g) Refried Beans (page 67) or 3 cups (455 g) Picadillo (recipe follows)

For baking (*choose one*)
Salsa Roja or Ranchera (page 50)
or
Refried Beans (see Enfrijoladas, page 80)

Stuffed Chiles

Chiles rellenos
Photo p. 167

In Mexican kitchens, salsas are the most common application for chiles, but the next most common one is stuffing. Chiles rellenos (*relleno* = filled or stuffed) can be a main course or an appetizer. They can be stuffed with meats, seafood, vegetables, beans, cheese, or anything really. The fresh chile most often used for stuffing is the poblano because of its large size and flavor: It is relatively mild, and earthy and meaty. The dried chile most commonly stuffed is also the poblano, and when it is dried, it is called *chile ancho*. Although these particular chiles are used throughout Mexico, they are most popular in the central regions. Every region has their favorite stuffing chile.

———

For the fresh chiles: Place the chiles over a high open flame, and using tongs, turn constantly making sure every surface of the chile is charred and black. Place in a plastic bag and wrap them in a cloth. Let them sit for 5–10 minutes. The steam inside the bag will finish peeling and start cooking the chiles. Remove from the bag and peel off the charred skin. (Do not do this under running water or you will lose all of the flavor.) Make a lengthwise slit starting at the top of the chile and remove the seeds and ribs. Do not remove the stem; it holds the chile together. Do not rinse them.

For the dried chiles: Toast the chiles on a hot frying pan or comal until fragrant, 1–2 minutes per side. Be careful not to burn them or they will get bitter. Place in a bowl and cover with hot tap water. Let rest for about 10 minutes until soft. Make a lengthwise slit starting at the top of the chile and remove the seeds and ribs. Do not remove the stem though; it holds the chile together.

Stuff the chiles: Stuff the chiles with your desired filling. Place in a baking dish in a single layer. Bake on their own or cover with salsa or refried bean sauce. If using refried beans, thin with hot water until runny before adding to the baking dish. Bake until the sauce is bubbling and the stuffing is heated through, about 10 minutes.

Picadillo
Picadillo

Preparation time
10 minutes
Cooking time
35 minutes
Makes
about 4 cups (600 g)

4 tablespoons lard or vegetable
  oil
1 small onion, finely diced
4 garlic cloves, finely chopped
1 lb (455 g) ground (minced)
  beef
1 lb (455 g) ground (minced)
  pork
Salt
1 tablespoon dried Mexican
  oregano
3 cloves, ground
4 allspice berries, ground
1 small (2-inch/5 cm) Mexican
  cinnamon stick
2 lb (910 g) plum tomatoes,
  finely diced
½ cup (45 g) sliced (flaked)
  almonds
½ cup (80 g) raisins

In a large pot, heat the lard or oil over medium-high heat. Add the onion and garlic and cook until translucent, about 5 minutes. Add the meats and cook, breaking them up with a wooden spoon, until cooked through and broken down, about 10 minutes. Season with salt. Add the oregano, ground spices, and cinnamon stick. Add the tomatoes, reduce the heat to low, and simmer until the tomatoes are a brick color and their liquid has evaporated, about 10 minutes. Add the almonds and raisins and season to taste with salt. Cook until the flavors meld and the raisins are plump, about 5 more minutes; set aside. Remove the cinnamon stick. Cool to room temperature. Use right away or store in an airtight container in the refrigerator for up to 1 week or the freezer for up to 1 month.

Preparation time
20 minutes
Cooking time
35 minutes, plus salsa
prep time
Serves 6

GF VEG

For the flautas

2 lb (910 g) Yukon Gold
  potatoes, scrubbed
1 lb (455 g) quesillo (Oaxaca
  string cheese), pulled
½ cup (115 g) crema or
  crème fraîche
2 teaspoons salt, plus more
  to taste
12–16 Fresh Tortillas (page
  24)
Vegetable oil, for shallow-
  frying

For serving

½ cup (115 g) crema or
  crème fraîche
1 cup (125 g) crumbled
  queso fresco
1 small head iceberg lettuce,
  finely shredded
1 cup (240 ml/8 fl oz) Raw
  Salsa Verde (page 46), or
  salsa of your choice

Crispy Potato and Quesillo Flautas

Flautas de papa y quesillo

Flautas, or flutes, which are named after their shape, are a perfect leftover dish. Whenever you have stale tortillas and some chicken, cheese, or mashed potatoes, this is a great solution to breathe new life into them. Stale tortillas are actually better for frying than fresh tortillas.

We combined the potatoes with cheese and cream to make them richer, but feel free to adjust the filling to your taste.

———

Make the flautas: Preheat the oven to 375°F (190°C/Gas Mark 5).

Place the potatoes on a baking sheet and bake until easily pierced with a sharp knife, about 30 minutes.

Mash the potatoes with the skin on and mix with the *quesillo,* crema, and salt. Season with more salt, if desired.

Place 2 tablespoons of the potato mixture in the center of a tortilla and roll very tightly, using toothpicks (cocktail sticks) to help keep it from coming undone. Make as many *flautas* as the filling allows.

Pour 1 inch (2.5 cm) oil into a large cast-iron pan and heat over high heat until very hot but not smoking (360°F/180°C). Fry the flautas until crispy and golden brown, 3 minutes

To serve: Remove the picks from the flautas. Serve topped with *crema,* queso fresco, and iceberg lettuce. Serve with the salsa alongside.

Preparation time
20 minutes
Cooking time
1 hour
Serves 6–8

⬛DF ✪GF

For the tongue
1 beef tongue
1 onion, cut in wedges
1 head garlic, halved
3 bay leaves
½ teaspoon coriander seeds
2 ancho chiles, seeded
2 teaspoons salt

For the tacos
1 cup (140 ml/8 fl oz) Bone Marrow Salsa (page 58)
1 cup (40 g) chopped fresh cilantro (coriander) leaves
Key Lime wedges, for serving
1 white onion, finely chopped
24 (or more) fresh Tortillas (page 24)

Tongue Tacos

Tacos de lengua

Tongue tacos are a classic street taco. We added a twist by frying the tongue in Bone Marrow Salsa (see page 58) for another layer of richness and spice. This is a great dish for a large group. You can make it ahead of time and when ready to serve, just fry the tongue, heat the tortillas, and impress your guests.

———

Cook the tongue: In a large pot, combine the tongue, onion, garlic, bay leaves, coriander seeds, and ancho chiles. Add water to cover by at least 1 inch (2.5 cm). Bring to a boil and cook for 15 minutes, then reduce the heat to a simmer and cook for 45 minutes. Add the salt. Remove from the heat and let the tongue rest in the liquid for 20 minutes. When cool enough to handle but still hot, remove the tongue from the liquid and peel the outer layer with your hands. Cut the tongue into 1-inch (2.5 cm) pieces.

Prepare the tacos: Place a large cast-iron frying pan over high heat. Add the bone marrow salsa and tongue and fry until golden brown, about 5 minutes. Transfer to a serving container or vessel.

Set out the tongue along with separate bowls of cilantro (coriander), onion, and Key limes. Set out the tortillas and let everyone assemble their own taco.

Preparation time
10 minutes
Cooking time
1–2 hours, plus salsa
cooking time
Serves 8–10

▌DF ✿GF

3 tablespoons vegetable oil
1 bone-in picnic ham*
   (3–4 lb/1.35–1.8 kg)
1 large white onion, halved
3 bay leaves
1 head garlic, halved
2 teaspoons salt, plus more
   to taste
2 lb (910 g) purslane
4 cups (950 ml/2 pints)
   Cooked Salsa Verde
   (page 48)

1 cup (20 g) epazote leaves
Fresh Tortillas (page 24),
   for serving

*Picnic ham is pork
   shoulder with part of the
   shank bone

Stewed Pork and Purslane
Puerco con verdolagas

This is the meat-lover's favorite way to eat veggies. The stew is typically cooked in a *cazuela* or clay pot and served as a main course alongside White Rice (page 70) and Basic Beans (page 64) with freshly made tortillas. As a vegan alternative, you can make this dish without the pork and add potatoes and *nopales* instead.

Purslane, *verdolagas,* is a meaty, tart green that holds its shape in stews. Finding fresh *verdolagas* and good-quality pork is key for this dish.

———

In a large pot, heat the oil over medium-high heat. Sear the meat on all sides until brown, about 15 minutes. Transfer to a plate. Add the onion, bay leaves, and garlic to the same pot and stir until coated with oil. Let them cook, stirring occasionally, until browned all over, about 10 minutes. Return the meat to the pot. Add the salt and water to completely cover. Cook over medium heat, covered, until the meat is fully cooked and almost fork-tender, 1–2 hours.

Clean the purslane of any brown spots or wilted leaves. Remove the toughest part of the stems and the roots, picking only the tender stems and all the leaves. Rinse under cold water and dry in a salad spinner.

Transfer the meat to a large plate or carving board. Strain and reserve the broth. Working around the bone, break the pork shoulder into 1–2 inch pieces. Discard the bone.

In a large pot, preferably clay, heat the salsa verde over medium heat and bring to a simmer. Cook until it reaches the consistency of applesauce, 5–10 minutes. Add the pork, about 2 cups (475 ml/16 fl oz) of the pork cooking broth, the purslane, and epazote. Adjust the consistency with more pork broth if necessary. It should be soupy but not watery. Cook until the purslane turns a darker shade of green but still has a bite, about 10 minutes. Season to taste with salt. Serve in a casserole at the center of the table with tortillas on the side. Leftovers can be stored in an airtight container in the refrigerator for up to 3 days.

Preparation time
15 minutes, plus overnight brining time

Cooking time
5+ hours

Makes
about 8.5 lb (4 kg) carnitas

⚫DF ⚫GF

For the brine
Ratio: 1 cup (230 g) coarse salt for every 1 gal (3.8 liters) water
1 suckling pig (11 lb/6 kg), cut into 7–9 pieces

For the carnitas
3 large heads garlic, halved horizontally
1 large bunch fresh thyme
6 oranges, thickly sliced
10 lb (4.53 kg) Lard (page 134)

For serving
Key lime wedges
Roughly chopped white onion
Fresh cilantro (coriander) leaves
1 cup Raw Salsa Verde (page 46)
Chicharrón (optional; page 132)
Fresh Tortillas (page 24)

Carnitas

Carnitas

Carnitas are a *taquería* staple, and everyone has their favorite. Ask for a recommendation for where to get them and you will get as many answers as people you asked. It is a phenomenal party dish and always a crowd pleaser and relatively easy to make, if you have time on your hands. Although carnitas take a while to cook, they are worth it. You can also make them in a smaller batch in a slow cooker using a pork shoulder. Just reduce the ingredients proportionally based on the weight of the pork. You can use a smaller bone-in cut of pork, instead of suckling pig, such as a shoulder.

Brine the pork: Pick a large container that comfortably fits the suckling pig pieces. Make enough brine to fully cover the pork by dissolving the salt in the water and keeping the proportions listed above. Refrigerate the pork in the brine overnight.

Make the carnitas: Remove from the brine and pat dry. In a big pot, preferably clay, arrange the pork. Add the garlic, thyme, and oranges and cover with the lard. Cook over low to medium heat for at least 5 hours, or until the meat detaches from the bone easily. If the lard smokes, reduce the heat. Alternatively, you can use a slow cooker.

Remove the meat from the pot piece by piece. Pull the meat from the bones and chop.

To serve: Serve the carnitas accompanied by Key limes, onion, cilantro (coriander), salsa, chicharrones (if using), and warm tortillas.

Preparation time
20 minutes
Cooking time
2 hour 30 minutes
Serves 10–12

ᛝDF ✌GF

For the guajillo adobo
12 guajillo chiles, seeded
3 whole cloves
2 allspice berries
1 tablespoon dried
   marjoram
3 tablespoons dried
   Mexican oregano
2 large white onions,
   roughly chopped
4 plum tomatoes
3 garlic cloves, unpeeled
4 tablespoons grapeseed oil

For the barbacoa
1 lamb shoulder (about
   6 lb/2.72 kg)
1 large white onion, halved
3 carrots, peeled and
   roughly chopped
3 garlic cloves, peeled
2 sprigs fresh epazote
1 handful (about 100 g)
   avocado leaves, fresh or
   dried
1 agave leaf (optional),
   charred
Salt

For serving
½ cup (20 g) chopped fresh
   cilantro (coriander)
½ cup (80 g) chopped white
   onion
Avocado slices or Herb
   Guacamole (page 130)
Mixe Chile Salsa (page 48)
Lime wedges
Fresh Tortillas (page 24)

Barbacoa

Barbacoa

Although most common in the north, barbacoa is made all over Mexico with regional variations. The lamb is traditionally cooked in a pit using hot coals and stones. A pot with the vegetables, herbs, and water rests on the bottom of the pit, a rack is placed on top, and the meat lies on top. It is covered with agave leaves and entirely buried. The drippings of the lamb flavor the broth, and the broth provides moisture for the lamb. It is then dug out and the broth is served in bowls, while the barbacoa is eaten in tacos. We have adapted the recipe for the stovetop, but you could cook it on a grill (barbecue), using a roasting pan for the broth and placing the lamb on a roasting rack on top. Just cover it with agave leaves and foil. This one, with avocado leaves, is a more Oaxacan version.

———

Make the guajillo adobo: In a frying pan or comal over high heat, toast the chiles, spices, and herbs, stirring, until fragrant, 1–2 minutes. Set aside. Place the onions, tomatoes, and garlic on the pan and cook until charred on all sides, about 10 minutes. Remove from the pan. Peel the garlic.

In a medium pot, heat the oil over high heat. Add the toasted and charred ingredients and cook until the tomatoes get mushy, 4–5 minutes. Add enough water to barely cover the ingredients and simmer until the liquid evaporates almost completely, 15–20 minutes. Transfer to a blender and blend to a smooth paste. Set aside.

Make the barbacoa: In a large pot, combine all the ingredients but the salt. Add water to cover by at least 1 inch (2.5 cm). Season with salt. Simmer, covered, until the lamb is tender, 1½ –2 hours, skimming the top to remove impurities, adding water if necessary.

To serve: Transfer the lamb to a serving bowl or platter. Break it up into smaller chunks and rub with half of the guajillo adobo. Strain the broth and add some to the lamb. Add the rest of the adobo to the broth. Serve in bowls for each guest with the garnishes and enjoy the barbacoa in tacos.

Preparation time
15 minutes
Cooking time
1–1 ½ hours
Serves 10–12

🍃DF ✵GF

4 tablespoons vegetable oil
2 lb (910 g) beef chuck or
  round (topside), cut into
  2-inch (5 cm) pieces
1 large white onion, halved
6 large garlic cloves, peeled
5 bay leaves
4 black peppercorns
2 tablespoons salt, plus
  more to taste
2 Yukon Gold potatoes,
  thinly sliced
2 serrano chiles, minced

2 lb (910 g) miltomates or
  tomatillos (the smaller the
  better), husked and rinsed
½ cup (20 g) chopped fresh
  cilantro (coriander)
White Rice (page 70), for
  serving
Fresh Tortillas (page 24),
  warmed, for serving

Beef and Tomatillo Stew

Entomatado de res

This dish is like preparing a chunky salsa verde straight in the stew. We use *miltomates* or *tomatillos de milpa*: These are heirloom tomatillos that tend to be smaller and darker in color, with a more concentrated flavor. You can sometimes find them at farmers' markets, or you can use regular tomatillos instead. Choose any cut of beef, but we use a fatty and flavorful cut, like chuck or round (topside). Use any leftover broth as a base for other dishes such as White Rice (page 70) and Vegetable and Ayocote Bean Soup (page 96). Enjoy this dish with some rice on the side, to soak up the good juices from the stew, and warm tortillas.

In a large pot, heat 2 tablespoons of the oil over high heat. Add the beef and half the onion, half the garlic cloves, the bay leaves, peppercorns and 1½ tablespoons of the salt. When seared on all sides, after about 5 minutes, cover with a generous amount of water and cook, covered, at a high simmer or very gentle boil until the meat is fork-tender, about 1 hour.

Meanwhile, slice the rest of the onion and garlic. In a large cast-iron or clay pan, heat 1 tablespoon of the oil over medium heat. Cook the onion and garlic until translucent, about 5 minutes. Transfer to a plate. Add the remaining 1 tablespoon oil and fry the potatoes until light golden, 4–6 minutes. Add the serranos and tomatillos and return the onion and garlic to the pan. Cook, stirring constantly but careful not to break up the potato too much, until the tomatillo changes color to a darker green, about 15 minutes.

Scoop the cubes of cooked meat into the pan with about 1 cup (240 ml/8 fl oz) of its cooking liquid. (Save the remaining cooking broth to use in other preparations, like rice or soups.)

Bring the stew to a simmer, add the cilantro (coriander), and season to taste with salt. Serve with rice and tortillas on the side. Refrigerate leftovers in an airtight container for up to 1 week.

From the early days of the conquest of Mexico in the 1500s come stories telling us of the lavish sweet dishes that were prepared with honey, tree syrups, spices, and fruit pulps for the Aztec emperor Moctezuma. He sent candies, fruits, nuts, and seeds to the kings back in Spain. Mexico also introduced the vanilla bean and cacao to Europe, and now they are widely enjoyed around the world. The first crop to be imported into Mexico was sugarcane, which began to be successfully planted in 1524, just three years after the conquest. That sweet tooth seems to have endured for centuries.

Mexicans love fruits, candies, *nieves* (ice creams and sorbets), breads, and cakes. Throughout our history we have adopted new elements to our dessert cuisine: from fine candies traditionally created by Catholic nuns to pastries brought over during our brief French/ Austrian rule in the mid 1800s. Today, in most home kitchens, we cook with much less sugar and rely more on fruit juices and pulps, or alternative sweeteners like honey or agave syrup. You will notice that most of the recipes in this chapter have a strong fruit presence. However, no matter what we use as a sweetener, whenever we indulge our sweet tooth, we are instantly taken back to our childhood and family gatherings.

SWEETS

Preparation time
45 minutes, plus 1½ hours
rising time
Cooking time
15 minutes
Makes
10 rolls

♣VEG

For the crumble
1¾ sticks (7 oz/200 g) butter,
  at room temperature
¾ cup (150 g) sugar
2 vanilla beans, split
  lengthwise
2 cups (250 g) all-purpose
  flour

For the dough
1¾ cups (225 g) all-purpose
  (plain) flour
3 tablespoons sugar
Scant 1 tablespoon (6 g)
  active dry yeast
1 teaspoon salt
1 egg, beaten
scant ½ cup (100 ml/3.4 fl
  oz) whole milk
3 tablespoons (45 g) butter,
  at room temperature

1 tablespoon orange
  blossom water
Grated zest of 1 orange

Orange Rolls

Conchas de naranja

This is the dough used to make *conchas,* a classic Mexican *pan dulce* (sweet bread). However *conchas*—meaning "shells" in Spanish—require a special mold that shapes the crust into a seashell and it is hard to find outside of Mexico. We replaced the seashell crust with a crumble of the same dough. The crumble crisps up, providing an unexpected contrast in texture to the rich bread. If you'd like to eat this freshly baked for breakfast, you can make everything the night before, refrigerate, and just proof and bake the morning of. Enjoy with hot chocolate or coffee on the side or for dunking,

———

Make the crumble: In a stand mixer with the paddle attachment, cream the butter until pearl white. Add the sugar and cream for 3 more minutes. Scrape the vanilla seeds into the mixer. Slowly add the flour until barely incorporated; do not overmix. Wrap in plastic wrap (cling film) or place in a zip-seal bag and refrigerate for at least 30 minutes. Crumble the mixture before using.

Make the dough: In a stand mixer with the paddle attachment or by hand, combine the flour, sugar, yeast, and salt. Add the egg and milk and mix until incorporated. Slowly add the butter, followed by the orange blossom water and orange zest. Mix on low speed, scraping occasionally until the dough starts to pull away from the bowl. Turn the dough into a greased bowl and cover with a tea towel or cloth. Allow to rise in a warm place until doubled in size, 30–45 minutes. Turn onto a floured surface and divide into 10 equal balls, about the size of a golf ball (if available, use a scale to measure 30 grams each). If making ahead, refrigerate the rolls overnight or freeze, covered with plastic wrap (cling film), for up to 1 week. If baking immediately, place the rolls on a baking sheet and cover with a damp tea towel. Let rise in a warm place until doubled in size, about 45 minutes.

Meanwhile, preheat the oven to 325°F (160°C/Gas Mark 3). Top each roll with the crumble. Bake until golden brown, about 15 minutes.

Preparation time
25 minutes
Cooking time
1 hour, plus resting time
Makes
1 loaf (8–12 servings)

VEG

2 sticks (8 oz/225 g) butter, plus more for greasing the pan, at room temperature
4 tablespoons vegetable oil
½ cup (90 g) shaved piloncillo or brown sugar
1 teaspoon ground Mexican cinnamon
2 vanilla beans, split lengthwise
3 eggs

2 cups (500 g) mashed heirloom or baby bananas, completely black (it's okay if they are mushy)
Grated zest and juice of 1 Meyer lemon
2½ cups (600 ml/20 fl oz) whole milk
1¼ cups (150 g) cornmeal
2 cups (250 g) all-purpose (plain) flour, sifted

1 teaspoon baking powder
1 teaspoon baking soda (bicarbonate of soda)
1 teaspoon salt
1 cup (150 g) chopped walnuts

Banana Cornbread

Panqué de plátano y maíz

This is a loaf that brings two classics together, cornbread and banana bread, to make an even better bread. Warm up a slice, spread some fresh butter on it, and add a sprinkle of salt for one of the best possible treats.

———

Preheat the oven to 350°F (180°C/Gas Mark 4). Grease a nonstick 9 x 5-inch (23 x 12.5 cm) loaf pan with butter.

In a mixer with a paddle attachment, cream the 2 sticks of butter and oil until pearl white, about 5 minutes. Add the piloncillo and cinnamon and scrape in the vanilla seeds. Beat in the eggs, one at a time, beating well after each addition. Beat in the mashed bananas and Meyer lemon zest and juice. Add the milk and stir until incorporated.

Put the cornmeal in a large bowl and sift the flour, baking powder, baking soda (bicarbonate of soda), and salt into it. Add the flour mixture to the batter and mix until barely incorporated. Do not overmix. Fold in the walnuts and immediately pour into the loaf pan.

Bake until a skewer inserted into the cake comes out clean, about 1 hour. Let rest for 30 minutes before serving.

Preparation time
35 minutes
Cooking time
15 minutes
Serves 4–6

♣ VEG

For the cinnamon sugar
1 Mexican cinnamon stick
½ cup (100 g) sugar

For the batter
scant ½ cup (100 ml/3.3 fl oz) water
⅓ cup (80 ml/2.5 fl oz) whole milk
2 tablespoons heavy (whipping) cream
6 tablespoons (3 oz/90 g) unsalted butter

1 teaspoon sugar
1 teaspoon salt
1⅓ cups (180 g) all-purpose (plain) flour, sifted
4 eggs

For frying
Canola (rapeseed), peanut (groundnut), or other high-heat oil, for deep-frying (about 2 qts/1.9 liters)

Churros

Churros

As a kid, going for churros at the *churrería* was a memorable and unique family experience. As I got older, I lost the tradition—until I had kids of my own. I realized again how great churros are when I started taking my kids out for them. This is why we added churros to the menus of our restaurants, Pujol, Cosme, and Atla. They are simple and familiar, but we wanted to remind people of how much they love churros, and they really do. You can enjoy them with a fresh cup of coffee, Café de Olla (page 228), or hot chocolate, preferably Oaxacan.

Make the cinnamon sugar: Crush the cinnamon stick and grind in a spice grinder with 4 tablespoons of the sugar until a fine powder is formed. Combine with the remaining 4 tablespoons sugar. It can be stored in an airtight container indefinitely.

Make the batter: In a medium pot, combine the water, milk, cream, butter, sugar, and salt and bring to a boil, then remove from the heat. While still hot, whisk in the flour until smooth. Whisk in the eggs one at a time, whisking constantly until smooth. Transfer the dough to a piping bag, preferably fitted with a star tip (nozzle). Let the dough cool completely and refrigerate for at least 30 minutes. This can be done ahead and left in the refrigerator for up to 3 days.

Fry the churros: 20 minutes before serving, pour 2 inches (5 cm) oil into a deep pot (or deep-fryer) and heat to 350°F (177°C) on a deep-fry thermometer. Remove the piping bag from the refrigerator and pipe the dough directly into the hot oil in a spiral shape. For smaller individual portions, pipe in 4-inch (10 cm) lengths to make sticks. Fry until the bottom is golden brown, 3–4 minutes. Flip and cook on the other side until golden brown, about 2 minutes. Using a slotted spoon or spider, transfer to paper towels to drain. While still hot, toss in the cinnamon sugar and serve.

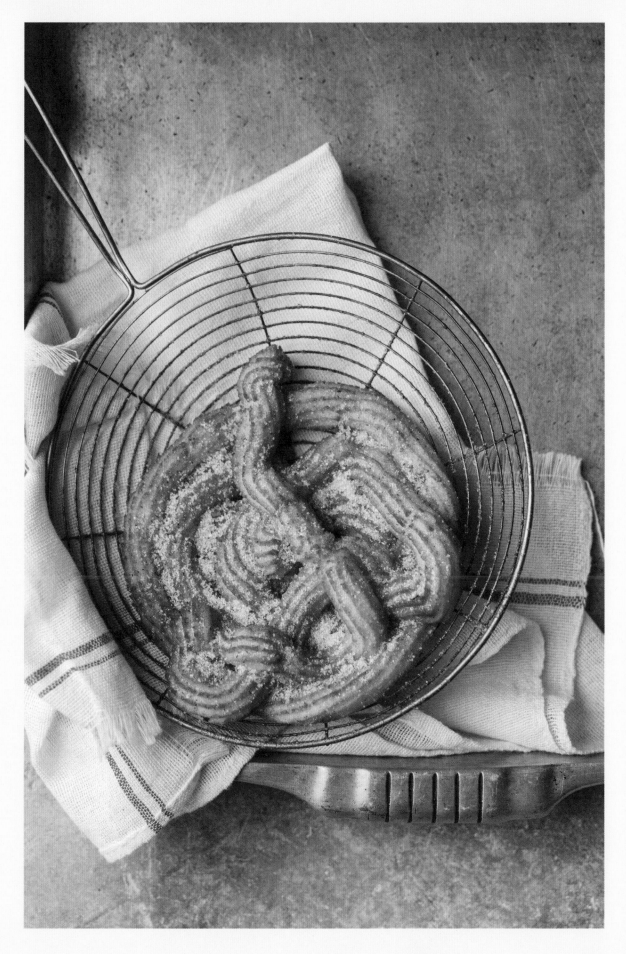

Preparation time
5 minutes, plus resting time
Cooking time
25 minutes
Serves 4–8

ᕼGF ✦VEG ▶30

2 cups (480 ml/16 fl oz)
  whole milk
4-inch (10 cm) stick
  Mexican cinnamon
Peel of 1 whole orange, in
  strips
½ cup (100 g) sugar, plus
  more (optional) for
  caramelizing
½ cup (45 g) freshly ground
  coffee
4 tablespoons cornstarch
Pinch of salt

Coffee Custard
Natilla de café

This recipe is inspired by Café de Olla (page 228). We decided to make the custard eggless by using only cornstarch to thicken. If you would like to make a vegan version of this dessert, you can also substitute a nut or seed milk for the dairy milk. The custards can be made ahead of time. Cover with plastic wrap (cling film) and refrigerate for up to 3 days, blotting the excess moisture off when you take them out to serve.

———

In a small pot, combine 1 cup (240 ml/8 fl oz) of the milk, the cinnamon, orange peel, sugar, and coffee. Bring to a simmer over medium heat.

Meanwhile, in a heatproof bowl, combine the remaining 1 cup (240 ml/8 fl oz) cold milk, the cornstarch, and salt, stirring to dissolve.

Strain the hot milk through a fine-mesh sieve (discard the solids). Then, whisking constantly, slowly stream the strained milk into the cornstarch mixture. Once it is fully incorporated, return the mixture to the pot and cook, whisking constantly to avoid clumping, until it is thick enough to see the bottom of the pan when stirring, about 20 minutes.

Divide the mixture among individual bowls or ramekins and let cool to room temperature. You can serve the custard as is, or if you have a blowtorch, sprinkle some sugar on top and caramelize it.

Preparation time
10 minutes, plus resting time
Cooking time
1 hour
Makes
1 pound (455 g)

⫶DF ⫶GF ⫶V ⫶VEG ⫶5

2 lb (910 g) ripe or overripe
   guavas, halved or
   quartered
1 cup (240 ml/8 fl oz) water
1 lb (455 g) piloncillo or
   brown sugar, plus more if
   needed

Guava Paste

Ate de guayaba

Ates are pastes made at the end of the fruit season when there is an abundance of ripe or overripe fruit. They are traditionally eaten with cheese on the side or as a candy by themselves, cut into squares. If you have one, this is best made in a copper pot, as it provides the best heat distribution.

In a blender, blend the guavas and water for about 2 minutes. Strain into a pot and add the sugar. Adjust the sugar based on the sweetness of the fruit. It should be as sweet as jelly. Cook over low heat, stirring often so the bottom does not scorch. Once you can see the bottom of the pot when stirring, after 45 minutes to 1 hour, pour into a mold, loaf pan, or your desired receptacle or vessel. Let cool to room temperature. Refrigerate overnight and unmold. Cut into squares or slices or serve as a block on a cheeseboard.

Preparation time
5 minutes
Cooking time
40 minutes
Serves 4–6

🍳GF 🍳VEG 🍳5

6 heirloom bananas or
   small plantains, ripe but
   not black, unpeeled
1 cup (230 g) crema or crème
   fraîche
1 cup (120 g) crumbled
   queso fresco

Baked Banana with Crema and Cheese

Plátanos horneados con crema y queso

This recipe shines for its simplicity. However, in order for it to be spectacular, the quality of the three ingredients really matters. Try to find heirloom bananas at a specialty or Caribbean store. The *crema* and cheese should also be from a good source. Or if you have good milk, you can replace the queso fresco with a homemade ricotta-style cheese called Requesón (page 82). If you are grilling (barbecuing), this is also a great dish to make on the grill. Place the unpeeled bananas on the cooler side of the grill and let them get black (for about 30 minutes). Regardless, enjoy the bananas while they are still hot.

———

Preheat the oven to 400°F (200°C/Gas Mark 6).

Place the whole bananas or plantains on a baking sheet and bake, turning them every 10 minutes, until the peel starts to split and the inside is tender when tested with a skewer, about 40 minutes. Remove from the oven but keep on the baking sheet. Carefully slice the peel lengthwise to just reveal the flesh and drizzle with some *crema* and sprinkle with cheese. Transfer to plates to serve individually, on a platter, or directly on the baking sheet on the table. Either way, people should carve out their own banana. Serve the remaining *crema* and cheese in bowls on the side, in case anyone wants more.

Preparation time
5 minutes
Cooking time
50 minutes
Serves 4–6

😋GF 🌱VEG

For the condensed "milk"
6 cups (1.5 liters) whey
   (from making 2 batches
   of Requesón, page 82)
4 tablespoons shaved
   piloncillo or brown sugar
1 teaspoon salt, or more to
   taste

For the sweet potatoes
About 1 cup (230 g) coarse
   salt, for baking (optional)
6 small (about 5 inches [13
   cm] long) sweet potatoes
Fleur de sel, for garnish

Roasted Sweet Potatoes
Camotes horneados

No matter where you are in Mexico City, as the night starts, you will hear a steam whistle in the distance. For an untrained ear, it might sound like a shift is ending at a factory, or the whistle of a passing train. For a Mexico City dweller, though, this invariably means that the *camote*—sweet potato—cart is approaching. The vendor keeps an assortment of roasted sweet potatoes in a barrel; they are kept warm by wood-powered steam that, when released, creates the unmistakable whistle sound.

Roasted sweet potatoes are meant to be a sweet treat and you can choose your topping, but the most common one is condensed milk. This recipe uses a byproduct of making Requesón (page 82) for our own take on condensed "milk." Try it out or use the store-bought canned one, but enjoy the sweet potato while it's hot!

———

Make the condensed "milk": In a large pot, combine the whey and sugar and cook over low heat until the whey is thick, about 45 minutes. There should be about 1 cup (240 ml/8 fl oz) of syrupy liquid. Remove from the heat and stir in the salt. Let cool to room temperature.

Meanwhile, bake the sweet potatoes: Preheat the oven to 350°F (180°C/Gas Mark 4). Line a rimmed baking sheet with plenty of coarse salt. The salt helps draw out the moisture from the sweet potatoes and seasons them. You can roast the sweet potatoes without the salt. Use parchment paper instead and be mindful of the bottom of the potatoes sticking to the parchment.

Place the potatoes on top of the salt and bake until they are soft when poked with a knife, about 45 minutes. Remove from the salt (discard the salt), dusting off extra salt from the skins. While still hot, slit open the top and pour some condensed "milk" on top and sprinkle with fleur de sel. You can either serve immediately or run under the broiler (grill) for 30–45 seconds until you see the whey brown a bit.

Preparation time
40 minutes
Cooking time
2–2½ hours
Makes
10–15 tamales

GF ✦VEG

1 large ripe pineapple
10–15 large dried corn
   husks, prepared (see
   page 36)
2 sticks (8 oz/225 g)
   unsalted butter, at room
   temperature
2 vanilla beans, split
   lengthwise
1¼ lb (565 g) freshly made
   white corn masa (page 22)

1 teaspoon ground Mexican
   cinnamon
1 teaspoon salt
1 teaspoon baking powder
½ teaspoon baking soda
   (bicarbonate of soda)

Pineapple Tamales

Tamales de piña

In Mexico City, street *tamal* vendors have *tamal de dulce,* or sweet tamal. It always has pineapple chunks in it but also raisins and a strong vanilla flavor. In addition to the classic pineapple chunks, we have added pineapple puree to the *masa* for a more intense flavor. Though we haven't included the raisins, you can add them if you like—just add them with the pineapple chunks—or any other dried fruits or nuts you would like. Enjoy this on its own for supper or breakfast, or serve as a dessert with whipped cream or ice cream.

———

Peel and core the pineapple. Roughly chop three quarters of the pineapple and transfer it to a large pot. Cut the remaining quarter into small cubes and reserve.

Set the pot over low heat and cook the pineapple, stirring occasionally so it doesn't stick or burn, until all the liquid is evaporated, and the pineapple is mostly broken down, about 1 hour.

Transfer half of the hot pineapple to a blender and blend until smooth. Return to the pot, mix to combine, and allow the pineapple puree to cool completely.

Soak the corn husks as directed in the Basic Tamal Recipe (page 36).

Meanwhile, in a stand mixer with the paddle attachment, cream the butter until pearl white, about 5 minutes. Scrape in the vanilla seeds. Mix in the masa, little by little, until completely incorporated.

In a small bowl, mix together the cinnamon, salt, baking powder, and baking soda (bicarbonate of soda). Add to the masa and butter mixture and mix to combine. Add the pineapple puree and mix for 2 minutes. Add the reserved fresh pineapple and mix until barely incorporated.

Divide the masa mixture among the husks. Wrap and stack the tamales (see pages 36–38). Steam for 1 hour 15 minutes.

Let cool at room temperature for 30 minutes, allowing to set before enjoying.

Preparation time
20 minutes
Cooking time
2 hours
Makes
8–10 tamales

✌GF ♥VEG

2 small butternut squashes
   (about 1 lb /454 g)
2 teaspoons salt
4 tablespoons honey, plus
   more for serving
8–10 dried corn husks or
   banana leaves, prepared
   (see page 36)
1½ sticks (6 oz/170 g) butter,
   at room temperature
1¼ lb (565 g) freshly ground
   white masa (page 22)

1 teaspoon baking powder
1 teaspoon baking soda
   (bicarbonate of soda)
Requesón (page 82), for
   serving

Squash Tamales

Tamales de calabaza

This *tamal* is both very Mexican and very New York. The late fall in New York brings with it a wonderful array of squashes and pumpkins and this recipe was born during that season. Squash is an ingredient that really ties both cultures together.

———

Preheat the oven to 350°F (180°C/Gas Mark 4).

Halve the squashes lengthwise and scoop out the seeds. With a sharp knife score a grid pattern into the flesh so they cook evenly. Place the squashes on a rimmed baking sheet, cut side up, and season with salt and honey. Cover with foil and bake until the flesh is soft and you can insert a knife easily, about 45 minutes. Let the squashes rest for 15 minutes still covered with foil. When cool enough to handle, but still warm, use a spoon to scrape the squash out of the skin into a bowl. The squash should be soft enough to become a paste just by stirring. Measure out 2 cups and set aside. Use the remaining squash in a salad or soup.

Meanwhile, prepare the corn husk or banana leaves as directed in the Basic Tamal Recipe (page 36).

In a stand mixer with the paddle attachment, cream the butter until pearl white, about 5 minutes. Mix in the masa, little by little, until completely incorporated.

In a small bowl, mix together the baking powder and baking soda (bicarbonate of soda). Add to the masa and butter mixture and mix to combine. Add the squash puree and mix for 2 minutes.

Divide the masa mixture among the husks or banana leaves. Wrap and stack the tamales (see pages 36–38). Steam for 1 hour 15 minutes. Allow them to set for 30 minutes.

Serve topped with *requesón* and a drizzle of honey.

Savory Squash Tamal: To serve this as a savory *tamal*, top with Salsa Roja/Ranchera (page 50), instead.

Preparation time
25 minutes
Cooking time
1½ hours
Makes
8–12 tamales

☆GF ❤VEG

6 fresh yellow corn cobs,
   reserving the husks
6 tablespoons (85 g) butter
1 vanilla bean, split
   lengthwise
½ cup (100 g) sugar
4 oz (115 g) freshly made
   white masa (page 22)
1 teaspoon ground Mexican
   cinnamon
1 teaspoon baking powder
1 teaspoon salt

For serving
1 cup (230 g) crema or
   crème fraîche, at room
   temperature
1 cup (120 g) crumbled
   queso fresco, at room
   temperature
Ground Mexican
   cinnamon, for garnish

Sweet Corn Tamales

Tamales de elote

This *tamal* draws inspiration from two places. First, from the *uchepo*, a type of *tamal* from the western state of Michoacán. Unlike most tamales, which are made with just masa, *uchepos* are made with the first fresh white corn of the season and barely any masa. Second, from American cornbread, which uses yellow corn (the most widely consumed corn in the United States). Fresh yellow corn kernels have more juice (or milk) in them, so we decided to add more masa to make the *tamal* set up well.

———

Cut the kernels off the cobs. Then, using the back of the knife, scrape the cobs to get as much of the milk out of the corn as possible. Measure out 2½ cups (365 g) of kernels and reserve along with the milk (discard the cobs).

In a mixer with the paddle attachment, cream the butter until pearl white. Scrape in the vanilla seeds. Add the sugar and mix for 2 minutes. Add the masa little by little until it is completely incorporated. Add the corn kernels and the corn milk and mix for 5 minutes so the corn juices incorporate completely. Add the cinnamon, baking powder, and salt and mix until incorporated, about 1 more minute.

Divide the mixture evenly among the fresh husks, wrap, and stack (see pages 36–38). Steam for 1 hour 15 minutes. Let cool at room temperature for 30 minutes to allow to set before eating.

To serve: Place a warm *tamal* on a plate. Slightly open the top. Add a dollop of *crema* over the *tamal*. Sprinkle with cheese and cinnamon.

Preparation time
10 minutes, plus 3–4 hours
   freezing time
Cooking time
5 minutes
Serves 6–8

Soursop Sorbet
(*Nieve de guanabana*)
½ cup (120 ml/4 fl oz)
   water
½ cup (100 g) sugar
1½ teaspoons
   unflavored gelatin
   powder (or 2
   bloomed gelatin
   sheets)
2 cups (500 g)
   guanabana pulp
   (strained of seeds)

**Passion Fruit Ice
Cream** (*Helado de
maracuyá*)
1 cup (240 ml/8 fl oz)
   whole milk
1 cup (240 ml/8 fl oz)
   heavy (whipping)
   cream
1½ teaspoons
   flavored gelatin
   powder (or 2
   bloomed gelatin
   sheets)

2 cups (475 ml/16
   fl oz) strained
   passion fruit pulp,
   fresh or store
   bought

**Blackberry and
Queso Fresco Ice
Cream** (*Helado
de queso fresco y
zarzamora*)
1¾ cups (415 ml)
   whole milk

4 egg yolks
⅓ cup (65 g) sugar
1 cup (145 g) frozen
   blackberries
Grated zest and juice
   of 1 lemon
1½ cups (200 g)
   crumbled queso
   fresco
½ teaspoon salt

Nieves and Helados

Since we have so many wonderful fruits in Mexico, there is a big tradition of making *helados* (ice cream) and *nieves* (sorbets). We tend to enjoy them at *neverías* (ice cream parlors) and town squares or plazas, purchased from the cart of a street vendor.

Although Mexican *helados* and *nieves* share the same principle with Italian gelatos and French sorbets, no complex appliances are required. In a wooden barrel full of ice and salt, a metal cylinder is inserted, and the mixture is constantly stirred in it until it becomes a frozen treat. Their textures lie somewhere between gelato and a snow cone, not as smooth as the former and not as icy as the latter. The advantage of the ice cream in a barrel is that vendors can continue to churn throughout the day even if they are out in a hot plaza.

In these recipes, we use a simple method that gives you the same texture—all you need is to clear out some flat space in your freezer.

ⅮF ❅GF ⏱5

Soursop Sorbet

In a pot, combine the water, sugar, and gelatin. Bring to a boil and stir or whisk until both are fully dissolved in the water.

Reduce to a simmer and add the guanabana pulp. Stir to combine and remove from the heat.

Pour onto a rimmed baking sheet or another rimmed container, filling it all the way across the bottom and let cool. Place in the freezer for 3–4 hours, whisking every 30 minutes, until you have a sorbet texture. Serve or transfer to an airtight container and keep frozen for up to 1 month.

❅GF ⏱5

Passion Fruit Ice Cream

In a saucepan, bring the milk and cream to a boil. Remove from the heat and whisk in the gelatin until it is completely dissolved. Add the fruit pulp and continue whisking until completely incorporated. Pour onto a rimmed baking sheet or another rimmed container, filling it across the bottom and let it cool. Place in the freezer for 3–4 hours, whisking every 30 minutes, until you have an icy ice cream texture. Serve or transfer to an airtight container and keep frozen for up to 1 month.

Blackberry and Queso Fresco Ice Cream

In a medium saucepan, bring the milk to a simmer over medium heat, then remove from the heat. In a medium bowl, whisk together the egg yolks and sugar. Whisking constantly, slowly stream in the hot milk. Return the mixture to the pan straining it through a fine-mesh sieve and cook over low heat, stirring with a heatproof spatula, until the mixture coats the spatula, about 10 minutes. Let it cool to room temperature.

Transfer to an ice cream machine and churn until creamy. (Alternatively, transfer to a metal bowl that is sitting in a larger bowl filled with ice and salt, and stir until the mixture starts to freeze, changing out the ice as necessary.) The whole process will take about 45 minutes. You can also leave it in the freezer for intervals to help with the freezing (see Avocado Sorbet, page 208).

In a small bowl, combine the blackberries and the lemon zest and juice. Add the blackberry mixture, queso fresco, and salt to the ice cream mixture. Transfer to a plastic or metal container to freeze for at least 30 minutes so the ice cream sets.

Blackberry and Queso Fresco Ice Cream (pp. 204-206)

Preparation time
30 minutes, plus 3 hours
  freezing time
Cooking time
10 minutes
Makes
1 pint (475 ml)

⬧DF ✷GF ◗V ✚VEG

For the sugar syrup
1 cup (240 ml/8 fl oz) water
1 cup (200 g) sugar

For the sorbet base
3 avocados
½ cup (120 ml/4 fl oz)
  coconut milk
2 tablespoons Key lime juice
1 teaspoon salt
4 tablespoons crushed ice

For serving
Extra virgin olive oil, for
  drizzling

Avocado Sorbet

Nieve de aguacate

Although this is a sorbet, the avocado and the coconut provide so much creaminess it could be mistaken for ice cream. Enjoy on its own or use it as a side to other desserts. You can also top with chopped macadamia nuts or Marcona almonds. Although an unconventional choice, avocado tastes wonderful in a dessert.

———

Make the sugar syrup: In a small saucepan, heat the water and sugar over low heat, stirring until the sugar is dissolved, about 5 minutes. Cook until reduced by half, 10–15 minutes. Allow to cool completely. Measure out ⅔ cup (150 ml/5 fl oz) of the syrup for the sorbet.

Make the sorbet: Scoop the avocado flesh into in a blender. Add the sugar syrup, coconut milk, Key lime juice, salt, and ice and blend until smooth. Transfer to a plastic or metal container. Place the container in the freezer for about 3 hours, stirring or whisking at least every 30 minutes, until you have a creamy sorbet texture.

To serve: Serve the sorbet with a drizzle of olive oil on top. Store in an airtight container in the freezer for up to 1 month.

Preparation time
5 minutes, plus 2–3 hours
freezing time
Cooking time
15 minutes
Makes
about 30 paletas, depending
on your mold

♨GF ⌂5

5 gelatin sheets
2 cups (475 ml/16 fl oz)
  heavy (whipping) cream
2 cups (475 ml/16 fl oz)
  whole milk
1 cup (225 g) grated
  Mexican-style chocolate

Mexican Chocolate Ice Pops

Paletas heladas de chocolate

Paletas heladas, or ice pops (ice lollies), are quite popular in plazas and town squares in Mexico. They can be fruit based—with combinations such as mango and chile or cucumber and Key lime—or milk based, like this recipe. Chocolate is a decadent ingredient that feels fresh and bright when frozen. And Mexican chocolate is even richer, as it is ground straight from the bean along with sugar and cinnamon, sometimes with almonds or nuts. You can even combine a fruit base and a milk base by only filling the mold halfway with one base, letting it partially freeze, and topping it off with another base. This is a perfect dessert or treat to make ahead of time, so as not to worry about the day you are having people over.

———

Bloom the gelatin by placing the sheets in enough ice water to cover them and let them rest until they become completely flexible, about 5 minutes. Drain. In a saucepan, bring the cream and milk to a boil. Add the bloomed gelatin, whisking constantly. Whisk until dissolved and remove from the heat. Add the chocolate and stir or whisk until incorporated. Let cool to room temperature.

Pour the mixture into an ice pop (ice lolly) mold, add sticks, and freeze until fully frozen, 2–3 hours. Remove from the mold and serve. You can keep the ice pops frozen for up to 1 month, as long as they are in an airtight container or bag.

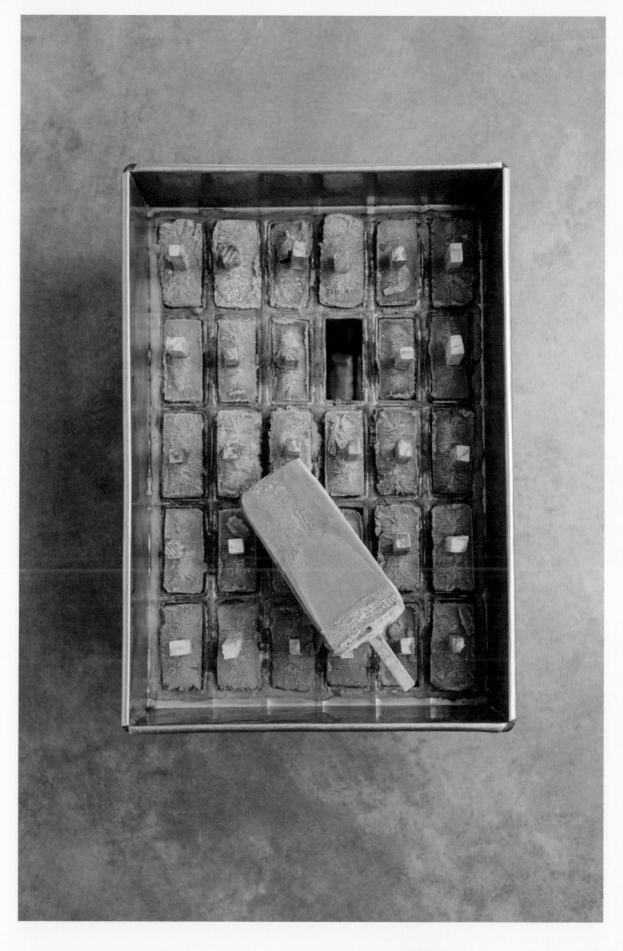

Homemade nonalcoholic beverages in Mexico are ever present. In addition to coffee, Mexicans always like to have a flavored drink or beverage to accompany meals. Carts on the street sell *atole*, a masa-based hot beverage, or fruit juices. And there are restaurant chains that only sell *aguas frescas*. We like to be drinking something throughout the day. Breakfast is unthinkable without a fresh fruit juice, *licuado* (smoothie), or an *atole*. Lunch begins with a tequila, mezcal, or a beer; maybe an *agua fresca* during the meal, and some sort of hot beverage at the end. We have a strong tradition of distilled liquors and beer and even a small but growing wine industry. In this chapter, we focus more on lesser-known nonalcoholic Mexican beverages that are consumed day in and day out, using fresh products.

We start with cold drinks and move into the hot drinks. Although nontraditional, we prefer to make all of these with very little or no sugar. There are conservative sugar amounts in the ingredient lists so you can get a truer idea of the flavor profiles, but you can of course adjust the sweetness level and type of sweetener to your taste.

DRINKS

Passion Fruit and Lavender Agua Fresca (*Agua fresca de maracuyá y lavanda*)
- 4 cups (950 ml/32 fl oz) water
- 1 Mexican cinnamon stick
- 2 cups (460 g) passion fruit pulp
- 1 tablespoon fresh lavender flowers
- ½ cup (100 g) sugar, or to taste

Red Prickly Pear and Meyer Lemon Agua Fresca (*Agua fresca de tuna y limón real*)
- 4 cups (950 ml/32 fl oz) water
- Pulp of 8 red prickly pears (about 2 cups) or 2 cups mixed berries
- Juice of 3–5 Meyer lemons, or to taste
- ½ cup (100 g) sugar, or to taste

Guava, Grapefruit, and Rosemary Agua Fresca (*Agua fresca de guayaba, toronja y romero*)
- 3 cups (710 ml/24 fl oz) water
- Juice of 3 grapefruits
- 2 cups (430 g) guava puree (preferably from fresh guavas)
- Leaves from 1 sprig fresh rosemary
- ½ cup (100 g) sugar, or to taste

Pineapple and Alfalfa Agua Fresca (*Agua fresca de piña y alfalfa*)
- 4 cups (950 ml/32 fl oz) water
- ½ large ripe pineapple, peeled and cored
- 1 cup (40 g) alfalfa leaves
- Juice of 5 Key limes
- ½ cup (100 g) sugar, or to taste

Aguas Frescas

I have always thought that *aguas frescas* were born out of resource-fulness. If you only have one melon to juice but there are ten people coming over for lunch, how do you make it yield more? By turning it into an *agua fresca*. It is a wonderful fresh tradition shared by the entire country. It is the perfect drink to have when a fruit juice would be too much and plain water too boring.

It has three basic ingredients: water, fruit, and sugar. The method is basically the same for all *aguas*. We have listed a basic method with four different ratios and flavor profiles, so you get familiar with the process and then make it your own. You can play with different fruit, herb, and spice combinations and by adjusting the sweetness levels to your taste and the ratio of water to fruit. For example, we like ours a bit more watery and I barely add any sugar. Following this one, we included three recipes for *aguas* that stray from the norm a bit and are each interesting in its own way.

In a blender, combine all the ingredients, except the sugar, and blend well. Standard blender jars probably won't fit all the ingredients so blend in batches. Strain through a fine-mesh sieve into a pitcher. Add sugar (or your preferred sweetener) to taste, adjusting for your own preference and based on how sweet the fruit is to begin with. Add enough ice to your liking. As an option, you can garnish with a piece of an ingredient in the agua. For example, a sprig of rosemary, a stick of cinnamon, or slices of lemon. Pour into ice-filled glasses.

1 avocado, halved
4 cups (950 ml/32 fl oz)
   water
½ cup (120 ml/4 fl oz) lemon
   juice or lime juice
½ cup (100 g) sugar, plus
   more to taste

Avocado and Lemon Water

Agua de aguacate y limón amarillo

Agua de limón, or Key lime water, is probably the most common *agua fresca.* This recipe is a fun spin on the traditional, using lemons instead of Key limes and adding avocado to acknowledge the very classic combination of citrus and avocado, but out of their normal context. Yana Volfson, our dear friend and restaurant beverage director at Cosme and Atla, came up with this recipe. We love it because it illustrates how working in New York has opened our horizons and expanded our palates. Before this, we Mexicans had never thought of an avocado as something you drink. Now, she has made us love it this way too.

————

Scoop the avocado into a blender. Add the rest of the ingredients and blend until smooth. Add more sugar to taste, if desired. Serve over ice.

1 cup (130 g) cashews
1 cup (185 g) brown rice
½ Mexican cinnamon stick
4 tablespoons shaved
   piloncillo or brown sugar,
   plus more to taste
4 cups (950 ml/32 fl oz)
   water

Cashew Horchata

**Horchata de nuez
de la india**

Horchata is originally from Spain and dates back to the Moorish invasion, more than a thousand years ago. In Spain, horchata has always been made with *chufa* or tiger nuts and even has its own denomination of origin. Horchata is also made throughout Latin America from a variety of seeds, nuts, or grains. In Mexico, however, horchata is always made with rice and cinnamon and occasionally we add some vanilla as well. The process for all horchatas is pretty much the same though, soaking overnight and blending into a raw milk the next day. This version by Yana Volfson mixes both the nut version and the rice version in what is a creamy, rich, and very satisfying drink. Our friend Yana adds rum, garnishes it with fresh mint, and serves it over crushed ice for a great cocktail she calls "Arroz con Rum."

———

In a deep container, combine the cashews, rice, cinnamon stick, 4 tablespoons sugar, and the water. Cover and refrigerate for at least 8 hours and up to overnight.

Transfer all of the ingredients to a blender and blend until smooth. Strain the mixture through a fine-mesh sieve (discard the solids). If desired, add more sugar to taste. Serve over ice.

Preparation time
10 minutes, plus overnight
soaking
Serves 4–8

DF GF V VEG 5

1 cup (130 g) cacao beans
5 cups (1.2 liters/2½ pints)
    fresh coconut water or
    good-quality bottled
    coconut water

Cacao
Water

Agua de cacao

This is really more of an infusion than an *agua fresca*. Although very simple to make, its flavor complexity is unbelievable, especially for how light it is. Although whole cacao beans are ideal—you can find them at a local spice store or specialty chocolate shop—cacao nibs work too. The important thing is to try to get the best quality possible for both the cacao and coconut water.

———

In a dry small saucepan or frying pan, toast the cacao beans until browned on both sides and fragrant, 5–8 minutes. In a large pitcher, combine the cacao beans and coconut water. Cover and refrigerate for 2 days. Strain through a fine-mesh sieve (discard the cacao beans). Serve over ice.

1 Mexican cinnamon stick
3 star anise
5 allspice berries
3 whole cloves
1 cup (240 ml/8 fl oz) water
1 piloncillo cone, shaved, or
   about 1 cup (190 g) brown
   sugar
Pinch of salt
Rind of 1 fresh pineapple
2 tablespoons white chia
   seeds

Tepache
Tepache

Tepache is an *agua fresca* made with fermented pineapple rind. It is wonderful not only because of its flavor but because you are using what would otherwise be scraps. So much of the pineapple flavor is stored in its rind, and through a simple fermentation you can extract all that flavor. Feel free to tinker with the spices and fruits. Though classic *tepache* is made with pineapple, it is also delicious with pear (see the variation below). Chia has been added to this version for more texture. Enjoy very cold.

―――――

In a small pot, toast the whole spices over high heat, stirring constantly, until fragrant, 1–2 minutes. Add the water, sugar, and salt and bring to a boil. Once the sugar is mostly dissolved, remove from the heat and let cool to lukewarm.

Place the pineapple rinds in a large vessel such as a pitcher, a deep clay pot, or a jug. Pour the spiced sugar syrup over the rinds and add more water until the rinds are completely covered. Cover the vessel opening with cheesecloth—you can tie it in place with twine—and allow to ferment at room temperature until there is foam on the surface and the texture of the liquid is slightly viscous, 2–4 days. Stir once a day.

Strain (discard the solids). Add the chia seeds, stirring occasionally for 15 minutes to avoid clumping, and then refrigerate for at least 1 hour and up to 1 week. You can adjust the sweetness up or down by adding more water or more sugar.

Serve over plenty of ice.

Pear Tepache: Replace the pineapple rind with 4 sliced pears.

2 young coconuts

Coconut Smoothie

Licuado de coco

This is a recipe where an ingredient just shines. The coconut becomes exquisite. Enjoy this drink as close to making it as possible over plenty of ice, preferably on a hot day. You can also use this *licuado* as the base to the Chia Pudding (page 86).

———

Open the coconut, save the water, and scrape the meat. In a blender, blend the coconut water and meat until smooth. Serve over ice.

Preparation time
5 minutes
Cooking time
25–30 minutes
Serves 4–8

ⓘDF ✪GF ◕V ♣VEG

3 cups (710 ml/24 fl oz)
   water
1 cup (240 ml/8 fl oz)
   coconut milk
3 cups (580 g) amaranth
   grain
½ cup (85 g) brown sugar
1 teaspoon salt
1 vanilla bean, split
   lengthwise

Amaranth Atole

Atole de amaranto

Atole is a nourishing, thick hot drink typically consumed in the mornings. It is usually made by adding masa to water. But other versions can be found, like with rice, which is fairly common, or amaranth, which is not so common. In rural areas, daily *almuerzo* (breakfast as we know it) happens at around 10 or 11 a.m. when eggs, tortillas, and beans are the meal. However, at dawn, before starting the workday, *atole* is consumed to fill up the stomach and give workers energy to tide them over until the *almuerzo*. This is called *desayuno* in rural areas (*des*= un, *ayuno*= fast, unfasting). In cities, *atole* is a popular alternative or complement to an early morning before-the-office breakfast. Serve hot and accompany with a *pan dulce* (such as Orange Rolls, page 184, or Banana Cornbread, page 186) or any of the *tamal* recipes on pages 198–202.

———

In a large pot, combine the water, coconut milk, amaranth, brown sugar, and salt. Scrape in the vanilla seeds. Bring to a boil and then reduce the heat to a simmer. Cook until the consistency is that of heavy cream, about 20 minutes. Remove from the heat and transfer to a blender. Carefully blend until smooth. Serve immediately or reheat in the pot if necessary.

Preparation time
5 minutes
Cooking time
25–30 minutes
Serves 4–8

DF GF V VEG

3 cups (710 ml/24 fl oz)
  water
1 cup (450 g) freshly made
  masa (page 22)
1 cup (190 g) brown sugar
1 cup (100 g) pecans
2 tonka beans
½ teaspoon salt

Tonka Bean Atole

Atole de tonka

This is a traditional *atole* recipe that has been tweaked and flavored with pecans and tonka beans. It is a play on the typical flavors of *atole*, such as vanilla or chocolate. Tonka beans are indigenous to South America, and we use them in Mexico because of their intense aroma and flavor that lies somewhere between vanilla and almonds. If you want to make a classic *atole*, remove the tonka beans and the pecans and add another ½ cup (450 g) masa. You can also blend in other spices, fruits, or nuts such as pine nuts or strawberries.

———

In a blender, combine the water, masa, and brown sugar and blend until smooth. Transfer to a medium pot. Add the pecans and tonka beans and simmer over medium heat for 20 minutes. Transfer to a blender and blend until smooth. Add the salt. Serve hot.

Preparation time
5–10 minutes
Cooking time
10–15 minutes
Serves 4–8

⬥DF ✹GF ◐V ✦VEG ▶30

8 cups (1.9 liters/2 qts) water
1 piloncillo cone, shaved
6 star anise
2 large Mexican cinnamon
  sticks
Peel of 1 small orange, in
  strips
1 cup (90 g) freshly ground
  coffee

Café de Olla
Café de olla

Café de olla, or pot coffee, is the ultimate party coffee because it can be constantly reheated and it will not lose its quality. You can actually make it ahead of time and reheat it when you need it. The coffee is spiced and sweetened, probably originally to mask the bitterness of coffee that has been on the fire for a while.

If you are not looking to make a big batch but would like to have a cup of *café de olla* in the morning, you can make a syrup with all the spices and the piloncillo, then strain it. Keep it in your pantry or refrigerator for adding to your regular coffee instead of simple syrup or other sweeteners. Enjoy hot with a piece of *pan dulce* (such as Orange Rolls, page 184, or Banana Cornbread, page 186). Or serve over ice with some milk in it.

In a pot, preferably clay, combine the water, piloncillo, star anise, and cinnamon sticks and bring to a boil. Once the piloncillo dissolves, add the orange peel. While boiling, stir in the coffee vigorously for 5 seconds as the coffee rises; remove from the heat. Cover and let sit for 5 minutes. Ladle right out of the pot and drink hot.

GLOSSARY

A la veracruzana. Veracruz is a state on the gulf coast of Mexico and where the Spanish settlements began. This preparation represents the cultural syncretism of Spanish and pre-Hispanic cultures. A basic tomato sauce is flavored with distinctly Spanish ingredients, olives, capers, and raisins.

Adobo. A thick salsa made with dried chiles, vinegar, and aromatics. It is typically used as a marinade or wet rub and differs from a normal salsas by the addition of vinegar. Like salsas, there are many varieties that get their name either from the chile used, from whatever will be rubbed with it, or from the region it was prepared in.

Agua fresca. A typical nonalcoholic beverage made by diluting fresh fruit juice with water and sweetening to taste. See page 214.

Anafre. A coal-fired grill, normally portable, that is the default cooking method for street vendors. A grill, pot, frying griddle, or *comal* is placed on top of it to cook various street foods.

Ancho. A key ingredient in most important dishes, it has a fruity earthy note and tends not to be spicy. The dry version of a *poblano*, it can be used for stuffing, or toasted and hydrated into sauces and stews. When purchasing, look for flexibility and a leathery texture. If they crack, they are not that fresh or have not been kept well.

Arbol. Can be found both fresh and dry. In its dry form, it is the most common dry chile in spicy salsas; it is consumed nationwide. It is long and bright red and seldom used for anything other than to provide spice in stews or salsas.

Atole. A hot beverage made by thickening water or milk and cooking a grain in it, typically nixtamalized corn in the form of masa. See page 226.

Botana. A snack. Small dishes or bites, or dishes meant to be shared as an appetizer, *botanas* are served at cantinas or at home before a meal. *Botanear* is the verb form for it and a very common activity in homes, restaurants, and cantinas throughout Mexico.

Chile. The spicy fruit of the sunshade family *Capsicum*. Originally from the Americas, it is now found worldwide in a large variety of sizes, shapes, colors, and heat levels. It is undoubtedly the ingredient that defines, characterizes, and makes Mexican cuisine unique. They are consumed both fresh and dried. Below are the most common or interesting varieties within Mexico:

Chile chilhuacle. A family of chiles—red, black, or yellow—harvested in the region of Cuicatlán, Oaxaca. Each of these gives a color to their namesake mole. Since they are rare, they are often substituted for *guajillo*, toasted to different depths.

Chile chiltepin. A small but potent chile. About the size of an allspice berry, it tends to grow wild in the *milpa*. It has different names depending on the area of the country. *Chiltepin* is common in the north, especially Sonora.

Chile chipotle. Dried and smoked version of a *jalapeño*. A popular choice because of its sweet and aromatic characteristics. Can be commonly found canned in *adobo*.

Chile Guajillo. Along with chile ancho, the most utilized chile in stews. It wields a bright red color when cooked. It is a smooth, deep red color and should be shiny and soft.

Chile Habanero. The spiciest chile in the country, and typical in southeastern salsas. Bonnet in shape, it can be consumed unripe (green and yellow) or completely ripe (orange and red), but it is always consumed fresh. Some people char it before using, and others add it directly to their salsas.

Chile Jalapeño. Along with *Serrano*, a common ingredient in Mexican kitchens and markets. Unlike *Serrano*, this chile is very versatile because of its larger size and meatier flesh. In addition to escabeche (see page 60–61), it can be used in salsas, stews—either cooked, raw, stuffed, etc.

Chile Morita. Although a common name in most of Mexico, *morita* slightly differs in shape and flavor from state to state. In general, it tends to be red berry-colored (hence its name) and can be used as a substitute to *chipotle*.

Chile Mulato. A cousin of *chile ancho*, *mulato* also comes from *poblanos*. However, it comes from those fruits that when ripe turn brown (instead of red, like *anchos*) and therefore have a deeper, earthier flavor. This chile is peculiar because it is always used in conjuction with another, normally *guajillo* and *ancho*, and rarely by itself.

Chile Pasilla. *Pasilla Mexicano*. Long and black, it gets its name from its wrinkly texture similar to raisins (*pasas*). It tends to be mildly spicy but has a very deep flavor. It is used in adobos, tables salsas, or stews such as the mole de olla (see pages 156–157).

Chile Pasilla Mixe. *Pasilla Oaxaqueño*. A unique smoked chile from the Mixe mountains of Oaxaca. Small and red, this chile is never found in its fresh form and is generally only found in the city of Oaxaca or in specialty stores. It is used for table salsas or stuffing.

Chile Piquin. Similar to *chiltepin* but pointier, they are both used in small quantities to impart a lot of flavor and spice, and are common in home gardens throughout Mexico.

Chile Poblano. A long, wide, deep green chile most commonly used for stuffing. Common outside of Mexico, this chile is undoubtedly one of the Mexico's favorites. In addition to stuffing it, it is used in soups, creams, and stews, and as a vegetable, cut into strips.

Chile Puya. Somewhere between *guajillo* and *arbol chiles*. Similar in shape and color to the former, it is spicy and smaller, like the latter. Some people call it *guajillo que si pica* (spicy guajillo).

Chile Serrano. A small, green (sometimes with red hues) chile used mainly for table salsas. It is said to have the perfect level of spice, and is therefore widely used.

Comal. A flat or almost flat surface made of a heat-conducting material that is placed directly on the fire. Although originally and most commonly made from baked clay, aluminium sheet or cast iron varieties are also used.

Crema. Cultured cow's milk cream with a higher fat content than sour cream but lower than crème fraiche. As a substitute, use crème fraiche or mix two parts sour cream with one part heavy cream.

Criollo. The word for heirloom in Mexico.

Elote. Corn cob or kernels in fresh form (versus *maíz*, which is used to describe the plant as well as the dried kernels).

Epazote. A wild plant endemic to Mexico that is, after cilantro, the most common herb used in Mexican cooking. It is almost always cooked (in stews and soups mostly) and rarely used raw. It has an earthy, bitter, skunky flavor to it.

Guisado. The word for stew in Mexico.

Hoja de aguacate. Avocado leaf. Used in the southern states of Mexico as an herb, prized for its earthy anise-y cinnamon-y intense perfume. Can be used in fresh or dried form.

Hoja santa. "Holy leaf." Found abroad as Mexican pepper leaf or root beer leaf, and has an anise-citrus-grassy flavor to it. It is always consumed fresh.

Jitomate (*Solanum lycopersicum*). The word for tomato in Mexico.

Limón. Lime. Although Persian or common limes are found in Mexico, the most common variety used is Key lime. Persian lime can be used as a substitute.

Maiz. The spanish word for Corn.

Metate. A flat volcanic rock over which food is pressed with a rod-shaped rock.

Milpa. An ancient method of agriculture in which symbiotic relationships are formed between the plants and their environment, similar to modern day permaculture. Consisting mainly of corn, beans, and squash, the *milpa* is a source of many other "wild" or unplanned ingredients such as *quelites*, herbs, or insects. In traditional agriculture, it is both the technique and the plot of land in which it is applied.

Miltomate. From the nahuatl words *milpa* and *tomatl*, *miltomate* is a small and intense variety of *tomatillos* that tends to grow wild in the fields. Deeper in flavor and with a purple hue, they are prized for their intense flavor.

Molcajete. Mortar and pestle made from carved black porous volcanic rock. Used to make salsas. See page 45 for seasoning instructions.

Mole. A category for typical Mexican sauces containing a combination of chiles, spices, and seeds/nuts. There are as many as there are towns in Mexico and they are typically prepared in festive occasions by the entire family. See page 124.

Molino. Mill. In food context, it typically refers to the machine used to grind nixtamalized corn, chocolate, mole, or other food products. The place where this machine is housed is also referred to as *el molino*.

Nahuatl. The Aztec language that is still widely used in the center of the country. Many of the words, especially related to food, that we use in Mexico now are etymologically tied to Nahuatl.

Nixtamal. The process—and the resulting product—of cooking dry corn in alkaline water, to loosen the pericarp and therefore be able to grind into a malleable dough. See page 22.

Nopal. The *Opuntia* cacti, or in food context, the paddles of any variety of this family. They are widely consumed both raw or cooked.

Pan dulce or pan de dulce. "Sweet bread." A category of sweet breads and pastries. Served with hot beverages in the morning or as a supper.

Pepitas. Hulled pumpkin seeds.

Quelites. Greens typically harvested wild in the *milpa*. Normally rich in nutrients, they are used in traditional cooking. There are hundreds of varieties, but some of the most common are lambs quarters, purslane, and watercress.

Quesillo/Queso Oaxaca. A fresh string cheese originally from the state of Oaxaca but now one of the most common cheeses nationwide, due to its melty, flavorful profile.

Queso fresco. A crumbly, fresh, slightly tangy and salty cow's milk cheese.

Taco. A tortilla with a filling, generally meat, inside. It is eaten with hands and typically served in street stands. See pages 172, 178.

Tamal. A steamed dumpling made with nixtamalized corn dough and a filling. It is either wrapped in banana or corn leaves and steamed. See page 34 for recipes and technique.

Taquería. The place where tacos are sold and probably the most common format of restaurant or stand in Mexico.

Tetela. A triangle-shaped pocket made with masa and stuffed with beans or cheese. See page 32.

Tlacoyo. An eye-shaped patty of *masa* and a paste filling. It is served with cactus salad or fresh salsa as a garnish.

Tomate/Tomatillo (*Physalis philadelphica*). A green plum-shaped fruit used to make salsa verde. It is tart and fresh but can be sweet when cooked.

Torta. In Mexican Spanish, a sandwich. Typically made with Telera (see page 114) or with bolillo, a baguette like roll.

Tortillería. The place where tortillas are sold and a common mom-and-pop business in urban areas.

Totopos. Fried tortilla chips, typically cut in triangle shape.

Zapote. A term for a soft, edible fruit from the Nahuatl *tzapotl*. There are several varieties, but all are cherished for their sweet flavor. They are some of the few fruits in season during the dry, hot months.

INDEX

ABOUT THE AUTHORS

Enrique Olvera

Enrique Olvera discovered his love for cooking in the kitchen of his grandparents' bakery in Mexico City, Mexico as a young boy. Knowing the challenges of working in the food industry, his family encouraged him to pursue a more traditional career, but Olvera insisted that he was "born to love food." His ambitions took him far from home to New York's Culinary Institute of America where his formal training began. Upon graduation, Olvera returned to Mexico City, and at 24 he opened his first restaurant, Pujol.

In addition to Pujol, Enrique Olvera is the chef/founder of the more casual Cosme and ATLA in New York City, Ticuchi and Eno in Mexico City, Criollo in Oaxaca, and Manta in Cabo. Fueled by a constant exploration of Mexico's ingredients and culinary history, passion for subtle flavor compositions, and deeply personal approach to the idea of simply cooking what you have, Olvera has become a leader in Mexico's new gastronomy.

Olvera published his first book, *Uno*, in 2010, in which he describes the philosophy behind his cooking and the state of the Mexican cuisine. His second book, *En la Milpa*, focuses on "la milpa," a Mexican agricultural technique where waste is minimized and everything serves a purpose—a practice Olvera takes very seriously. His first book with Phaidon, *Mexico From the Inside Out*, features recipes "defined by his dedication to detail and his fearless palate," as described by the *New York Times*.

Olvera's hard work has earned him international recognition and admiration. In 2015 he was the recipient of the Diner's Club International Lifetime Achievement Award for Latin America. Pujol currently ranks 13th on the prestigious list of the World's 50 Best Restaurants. His debut U.S. restaurant, Cosme, garnered international acclaim in its first year, earning a three-star review from the *New York Times*, a James Beard Award nomination for Best New Restaurant in America, and it sits at 25th on the 2018's World's 50 Best Restaurant list. The only chef with 2 entries on the top 50.

Luis Arellano

Luis Arellano is an experienced cook who preserves his roots in his creative spirit. He believes in simplicity above all else, and is a curious explorer of ingredients. Before opening Criollo, in Oaxaca, he was the Chef de Cuisine behind the acclaimed Casa Oaxaca, and subsequently the creative director at Chef Olvera's Pujol. He hails from a long line of bakers, inmersed in the food world since very young. He is undeniably inspired by the cuisine of his native Oaxaca—by its traditions and ingredients. But, in a spongelike manner, he has taken in a mixture of influences from his travels to create a unique cuisine.

Gonzalo Goût

In addition to his passion for food and beverage service, Gonzalo is a tireless researcher of food cultures of Mexico. Since he graduated from the Culinary Institute of America, he has worked with Chef Enrique Olvera on and off since 2009. In addition to working on both of his Phaidon books, he has been involved in numerous Olvera projects: the kitchen and dining room of Pujol, the Condesa DF kitchen, on the production team for Mesamérica, as a manager at Eno, as the opening general manager at Cosme, and most recently running Ticuchi as Olvera's partner.

Daniela Soto-Innes

Originally from Mexico City, Daniela Soto-Innes is the chef/partner of Cosme and ATLA in New York City. In 2014, she moved to New York City to open Cosme as Chef de Cuisine under Chef Olvera's helm and soon after was named the James Beard Rising Star Chef of the Year. Prior to joining Cosme, Daniela graduated from Le Cordon Bleu College of Culinary Arts in Austin, Texas and held positions at Brennan's and Underbelly in Houston. She believes that the simplest food can inspire the most imagination and makes her dishes meaningful by "finding the secret life in each ingredient."

Cooking Notes

Cooking times are for guidance only, as individual ovens vary.
If using a fan (convection) oven, follow the manufacturer's
instructions concerning oven temperatures.

Exercise a high level of caution when following recipes involving
any potentially hazardous activity, including the use of high
temperatures, open flames, slaked lime, and when deep-frying.
In particular, when deep-frying, add food carefully to avoid
splashing, wear long sleeves, and never leave the pan unattended.

Some recipes include raw or very lightly cooked eggs, meat, or fish,
and fermented products. These should be avoided by the elderly,
infants, pregnant women, convalescents, and anyone with an
impaired immune system.

Exercise caution when making fermented products, ensuring
all equipment is spotlessly clean, and seek expert advice if in
any doubt.

When no quantity is specified, for example of oils, salts, and
herbs used for finishing dishes or for deep-frying, quantities are
discretionary and flexible.

All herbs, shoots, flowers and leaves should be picked fresh from
a clean source.

Exercise caution when foraging for ingredients; any foraged
ingredients should only be eaten if an expert has deemed them safe
to eat.

Both metric and imperial measures are used in this book. Follow
one set of measurements throughout, not a mixture, as they are
not interchangeable.

All spoon and cup measurements are level, unless otherwise stated.
1 teaspoon = 5 ml; 1 tablespoon = 15 ml.

Australian standard tablespoons are 20 ml, so Australian readers
are advised to use 3 teaspoons in place of 1 tablespoon when
measuring small quantities.

Recipe Notes

All herbs are fresh, unless otherwise specified.

All cream is 36–40% fat heavy whipping cream unless otherwise specified.

All milk is whole at 3% fat, homogenized and lightly pasteurized, unless otherwise specified.

Kosher salt is Diamond Crystal (UK, please use flaked salt in its place).

All butter is unsalted.

Breadcrumbs are always dried, unless otherwise specified.

All chiles shoud be destemmed, seeded, and deveined unless otherwise specified.

Author Acknowledgements
To our ever-inspiring friends and families, thank you.

This book would not have been possible without the great support of our teams at Criollo, where most of the dishes were prepared and photographed. The teams at Cosme, Eno, Atla, and Pujol played a great part as well.

Thanks to Yana Volfson for being a beverage mastermind.

A big thank you also to Raul Cabra and Frederick Silva of Oaxifornia. To Sasha Correa, Jesus Durón, Ale Flores, Javier Garciadiego, Santi Guasti, Paty Hernandez, Larissa Lawrence, and Ana Odermatt for providing countless bits of feedback, information, and planning.

Phaidon Press Limited
Regent's Wharf
All Saints Street
London N1 9PA

Phaidon Press Inc.
65 Bleecker Street
New York, NY 10012

phaidon.com

First published 2019
© 2019 Phaidon Press Limited

ISBN 978 0 7148 7805 8
ISBN 978 0 7148 7978 9 (signed edition)

A CIP catalogue record for this book is available from the British Library and the Library of Congress.

Commissioning Editor
Emily Takoudes

Project Editor
Sanaë Lemoine

Production Controllers
Sue Medlicott and Nerissa Dominguez Vales

Photography
Araceli Paz

Design
Mucho

Printed in China

Phaidon would like to thank Vanessa Bird, Cecilia Molinari, and Kate Slate.